COME BACK, AMERICA

Evan Mecham

Printed by
BookCrafters Inc.
Chelsea, Michigan

Cover Design by
Louis Charpentier

Typography by
Hohm Inc.
Prescott Valley, Arizona

M P Press
P.O. Box 970
Glendale, Arizona 85311
(602) 249-1776

This unique book describes how one American endured the incarceration of a Nazi prison camp and came home determined to discover the real meaning of the greatness of America.....exciting.....I have warmly recommended it to all my friends.

Dr. W. Cleon Skousen
Author, International Scholar
Founder of The Freemen Institute

If you haven't met the real Evan Mecham you will meet him in the pages of this revealing statement of a strong man's convictions about the public service opportunities he finds so challenging. It is a "Made in the U.S.A." declaration of faith and commitment that is refreshing.

J. Howard Pyle
Former Governor of Arizona

I am especially pleased to see the plans which will make President Reagan's "New Federalism" work in our state.

Nonavie Dyer
Arizona Chairman,
Reagan for President

An excellent inside glimpse of Arizona politics positively presented.....The author is an obvious Constitutional authority and dedicated to uphold it!

Kenneth C. Chatwin
Judge, Superior Court,
Maricopa County, Arizona

Dedication

I dedicate this book to Florence: my best friend in life, most loyal supporter, a sympathetic and creative critic in all things, the perfect mother of our seven children. The credit for anything of value that I am privileged to contribute to my family and fellow man must be bestowed on her in equal measure. My fervent prayer is that I can prove worthy of her constant companionship of 38 years at this writing, through the remainder of this life and through Eternity.

Acknowledgement

Many people helped me prepare this manuscript through their influence on me, both positive and negative, from the Founding Fathers of America to a Nazi interrogations officer, political figures, and just good people. Here, I'd like to single out two who had most to do with actual publication.

—Dr. W. Cleon Skousen. I owe him a great debt of gratitude for enhancing my knowledge, understanding, and appreciation for the Founders and the Inspired Constitutional System of American Government. Dr. Skousen is one of the great men of our time and I have valued his friendship, association in The Freemen Institute and his generous permission to borrow freely from his work.

—Ronald Van Doren. A talented writer and author in his own right, he was the catalyst in refining my personal vision of America to a concise book form that would communicate what I wanted to the modern reader. He challenged my thinking and encouraged me to realize that I had a story worth telling and a responsibility to tell it.

TABLE OF CONTENTS

INTRODUCTION:
NEW FEDERALISM, NEW PROSPERITY

At the beginning of the 1980's the United States of America was in the throes of what future historians may call The Third American Revolution, a peaceful one to restore principles of government embodied in the Constitution.

This was the reaction of a people who still had a measure of freedom against a growing impotence, stagnation and defeatism of a great nation being led to the edge of bankruptcy — both moral and economic — by the same old forms of national Socialism. The desire to reverse the 50-year march toward oblivion was indicated in the election to the Presidency of Ronald Reagan in 1980. He represented our hope, perhaps a final one, for the survival of free institutions that historically made America the most powerful, creative, productive and abundant nation in history.

At this writing it remains to be seen whether we will actually reverse the trend, or continue to let Socialistic welfare statism grow until it destroys the incentive to produce. As production tumbles, the economy falters and then collapses, taking our waning political systems with it.

With this slim volume, I try to make my contribution to this revolt, pointing out from my experience how I came to be a constitutionalist and what can be done by Americans at whatever level of endeavor to save the nation and bring in a new prosperity.

This is not a scholarly treatise because I am not a scholar. I am a businessman and a student of my fellow man. I have learned many lessons, and I have the capability of applying what I have learned to the practical world. Within the limitations of space and time, I outline basic principles, point up mistakes that led to the crisis of the 80's and offer ideas of what can and should be done at the state level to most effectively dovetail with Mr. Reagan's New Federalism.

I believe the Constitution is the firm foundation, the bedrock, the heart, soul and fiber of America. It represents the rule of law instead of the rule of men. I think I speak for all constitutionalists that we do not intend to turn the clock back; rather, we are looking to the Constitution to get us back on the track so we can move forward once again. At the very least, the practical level, we have to say that efforts to develop an American Socialism haven't worked, just as Socialism hasn't worked anywhere else and is a miserable failure. We simply can't keep propping up and patching a house built on such insubstantial sand. We need the solid firmament the Constitution provides us.

The first American Revolution started in 1776 with the declaration of the rights of a free people to live in dignity and harmony with strength. It led to the establishment of the Constitution based in immutable natural law, practical politics and more than a little common sense.

The second revolution started in 1933 when, on the pretext of giving people something for nothing through social and fiscal manipulation, an autocracy was imposed by those who would become the ruling elite through a faulty social science. They seized power gradually, and through control of education perpetuated themselves with two generations of bureaucratic and scholastic clones.

The third revolution found voice in 1980 with the advent of the Reagan Administration. It had been long in coming. The bureaucratic rule had become entrenched years earlier.

By 1982, although badly mangled, the Constitution is still in effect as the basic law in the minds and hearts of most good Americans and it is our duty at the state and local level to help the Reagan Administration reestablish that law against an entrenched and illegal bureaucracy controlled by selfish interests.

We must:
1. Reaffirm the Constitutional guarantees to "life, liberty and the pursuit of happiness," and "...be secure in person and property."
2. Promote the proper separation of powers so clearly delineated by the Constitution between Executive, Legislative, and Judicial in the federal government.
3. Reestablish the areas of power, authority, and responsibility between the states, local, and federal levels as so clearly defined in the Constitution.
4. Effectively protect the common good and personal freedom against incursions contrary to the provisions of the Constitution.

Neither the Congress, nor the courts, nor the Executive branch of the federal government are empowered to break the clearly-stated Law of the Land, the Constitution. However, those three branches have chosen to infringe on those rights. Therefore, it is incumbent on the states of the

United States and other governments at the working level to secure those rights for all the people.

The success or failure of this revolution depends on the numbers and level of participation of those people who really understand the problems and are willing to lend a hand in their solutions. Everyone gives lip service to the desire for freedom, liberty, and prosperity. Whether or not you deserve it and obtain it may depend on your actions after reading this book.

I have great faith in the goodness and the common sense of the majority of Americans. Together I think we will make the corrections so badly needed in our government, our economy, and in our society. I believe that the next ten years will see America make the greatest comeback of any nation in history. That's why I have titled this book *COME BACK, AMERICA.*

CHAPTER ONE

**"There was an explosion in the belly of my P-51
and I didn't even see what hit me."**

Mine was one of four P-51 Mustang fighters escorting
an F-5 photo plane which was an unarmed P-38 Lightning
taking pictures of targets near a town called Ruhland in
what is now East Germany. It was March 7, 1945, toward
the end of World War II, and the Russian offensive was
overrunning the countryside from the East as ours moved
Westward. The photo plane had his pictures and we
headed back home, our mission being to protect the photo
plane which was the "eyes" of the 8th Air Force.

Our one problem and a big one at this time when the
Germans were virtually finished, was their new jet aircraft.
They really had us outclassed, able to climb faster than a
P-51 could go on the level. Before their jets came along the
unarmed photo planes flew without escort because a P-38
was the fastest in the world and could run from any at-
tacker unless they were caught off guard. The jets changed
that so we flew escort.

On this mission my radio had a bad problem with static
and I turned it down to wait until somebody talked before
turning it up. We kept radio silence unless attacked or
there was some other emergency.

I heard an excited shout. As I reached to turn up the
radio, I was too late.

"Blam!"

There was an explosion in the belly of my P-51 and I didn't even see who hit me. Our formation went in a quick turn and I had my hands full controlling my plane. I lost all engine power and my controls were shot up so I had to hold full right stick to keep the wings level. Immediately, I tried to head for Poltava which was our emergency base in western Russia. (I had an identity tag around my neck that was in Russian and had an American flag. It said I was an American flyer and offered a reward to deliver me to Poltava.)

I dropped my external fuel tanks, tried to work with the internal fuel system and nothing happened. My oil pressure was also zero so I knew my engine was gone. A P-51 without power glides only slightly better than a rock. I figured I would go as far as I could and then bail out. At 25,000 feet I could glide about 25 miles, bail out and try to hide until the advancing Russians, approximately 50 miles to the East, came through. I couldn't make it to Poltava.

All of this happened in seconds, although it seemed much longer. The mind can accomplish fantastic things in an emergency.

My plans were suddenly changed when fire started coming through the floor of the cockpit. It wouldn't be long before the internal fuel tanks full of 155 octane would explode like dynamite. I had to get out in a hurry. To get rid of the canopy (ejection seats didn't come until we got jets), unhook oxygen, radio, safety belt and harness, I had to let go of the stick, sending the bird into a spin.

The 51 had a vicious spin. It had a heavy engine and a very small tail so it wound up real tight and the centrifugal force held me in the seat so that I couldn't get out.

I last saw the altimeter was at 14,000 feet and it was really unwinding. As we used to say — it looked like I had bought the farm. The fire was coming up and I couldn't raise myself from the seat, unable to get out, knowing that 155 octane fuel we used to get 1600 horses out of the 12-cylinder engine was ready to blow.

"Well," I said to myself, "it's going to be over in a hurry."

No one ever thinks it will happen to him — always to the other guy! When faced with the reality of my situation, I wasn't afraid to die. My biggest fear was getting maimed and coming back home a cripple. I wanted to come back in one piece or not at all.

At that point, unable to get out, going down, down, I thought about my mother, what she would feel, being told that I had gone. She hadn't wanted me to go to war, or fly. When she gave her reluctant permission to enlist at 18, I assured her I would always be alright. Funny how that all came back right then and the desire not to hurt my mother made me resolve to get out of that seat. I said a rapid but fervent prayer and tried again to overcome the force that held me to the seat when suddenly the plane seemed to drop out from under me — and I hit something hard and tumbled freely in the air. Apparently it was the tail hitting my knee. Breaking out of the clouds I pulled the ripcord on my chute and it opened. Hanging up there, the 51 gone and the trouble and noise past me, I was in complete peace and silence, no wind, nothing, the only trouble being that knee. I was still quite high. I saw no sign of where the plane hit so it must have exploded into small pieces.

The country below was beautiful. Forests all around, green valleys, but I knew I wasn't going to land in Russian-held territory. I thought, "Well, I'll make it into one of those little forests."

My leg hurt terribly by now. I twisted and adjusted the shrouds of the chute like we had been told to do to land with the wind. Luck was really with me. I was going backwards and, before I knew it, it seemed like the earth came up and hit me — heels first and rolling up on the back of my head. My whole body took the shock without being hurt. I was fortunate. I got rid of the chute and started to run for cover, but I couldn't get up. Looking around I saw a lot of people converging on me, some of them in uniforms and with rifles.

As the first two got to me, I just took my .45 out of the shoulder holster, tossed it on the grass, and put up my hands. I knew I wasn't going to get away from anybody. One of them grabbed me and held me from the back, another pulled a switchblade knife and held it out to me as though he was going to start cutting. It was then that I regretted surrendering the .45. If I had to go, I thought, it shouldn't be like this. With my good leg I got the man with the knife in the stomach and knocked him down and wrenched free. They backed off and we waited for the others to come up. Luck was still with me. A guy in uniform took charge. The switchblade was gone. A rifle with bayonet was behind me, indicating I should get up and go. I mean the blade was right at my buttocks. Right there I found out that despite the pain I could walk.

From the field I was marched to a local pub which seemed to be the center of everything. I still remember how incredibly beautiful that countryside was, all green and peaceful, untouched by the war. I was to see, days later, something that was more unbelievable — the devastation we had wreaked on the heart of Germany.

At this point I was with local militia people. I couldn't speak a word of German and they spoke no English. I had been marched several miles on what I was later to find out was a fractured knee. It had swollen and stiffened and hurt so much that I felt I was at the point of passing out. What saved me were items from my "escape kit" which included some emergency rations (I was allowed to keep those) and some pills. I think they were Benzedrine. We had been warned not to take those until we were almost spent; warned, also, that they would make you feel like taking on the whole German army.

I felt better. A German officer sat behind the desk in the pub and I sat down in the chair in front of him. A big soldier grabbed me by the neck and tried to stand me up. "Offizier, offizier!" he shouted to me, indicating I should stand in the presence of a superior. I pointed a finger at my chest and said, "Offizier, offizier," and sat back down. Almost respectfully, he left me alone.

There were telephone calls, conferences. It was surprising how rigidly the Germans followed their rules even at this sad stage of imminent defeat. That rigidity wound up saving me from what would surely have been a great deal of unpleasantness. Even not knowing the language, I could tell that there were rules and regulations for handling Prisoners of War and they were trying to follow them precisely.

By truck, I was transferred to an airfield I recognized having seen from the air as being near Ruhland. This time I was interrogated by an officer who knew very little English. They then put me in a cell for several hours and then moved me to the dispensary where the man in charge spoke English very well. A buxom young nurse dressed my knee while we talked. He was quite pleasant.

"How old are you?" he asked.

"Twenty," I replied.

"A shame," he said, "what a shame. You should be in school instead of fighting this stinking war."

He hated the English. He had been their Prisoner of War and then repatriated as a non-combatant.

"It should be us and the Americans and we'd take care of those English and French and Russians."

From there, and it took hours, I was driven in the back of an old pickup to Stalag 7-B where there were a lot of prisoners, some of them British captured at Dunkirk — five years before. They seemed finished, mentally and physically, and it took eight of the prisoners, the strongest among them, to carry me on a stretcher to the infirmary. The guys were underfed and weak.

I'll never forget one kid.

"When were you last in London, Yank?" he asked.

"Day before yesterday," I said.

"Is it still there?"

And I said, "Yeah, chopped up a little bit. The V-1's and 2's, they've taken chunks out of it but it's still okay and we're winning."

He cried for hours, couldn't stop sobbing, just at the idea that London was still there after all the hell he had gone through personally. He was a human wreck, unable to hold down food, about finished, and I pray he lived.

One of the guys who had carried me to the infirmary was a raw-boned type from Kansas.

"Ain't this something?" he said. "You know, time was when I wouldn't have needed any help to carry you. I'd just picked you up myself and carried you in my arms for as long as we had to go."

In the morning we had something we called "acorn coffee." It was hot so that was alright. About mid-morning we'd get what they called "cereal" — a teaspoonful of grain in more hot water. In the afternoon it would be a crust of hard bread you would have to put in water or suck on to make it edible. At night we had some vegetable soup, colored water actually, with pieces of vegetables floating in it, some rotten, some not; awful stuff to a newcomer like me who wasn't starving yet. But the kid next to me could eat anything. I gave what I couldn't eat to him.

I mentioned the rigidity of the Germans. The Luftwaffe's interrogation center for captured flyers was all the way across the country near Frankfurt, and I was sent there after six days at Stalag 7-B. This meant being on a train for three days and three nights in the darkest days of Germany's war. I was petrified all the time just thinking about getting shot by a .50 caliber burst from one of our fighters. We P-51 pilots liked nothing better than going down to the deck to strafe a train. Fortunately for me, that train was never attacked.

On that trip I saw what had happened to Germany. Before, from the air, I couldn't really experience the ruin and desolation. Even if I had known my geography then I could not name the places we went through because they just weren't there; we had blown them away. There were no stations, no restaurants, no towns worth calling that, and no food except what people carried on them.

I had two big guards who were, ridiculously, armed to the teeth when my left leg was in a cast and I had no crutches. I could only move about by putting my arms around their necks — one on each side, and hop along on my good leg. The second day they shared some hard bread with me. At one stop, they managed to get me watery soup which I had to wolf down because a German was ready to grab the bowl from me. I was relieved to get safely to

Frankfurt but apprehensive about what I would be put through in Dulag Luft — the Luftwaffe interrogation center.

My solitary cell was just large enough for the bed and room to open the door. One slit next to the ceiling let in some light. The bed was slats of wood with two blankets to roll up in, just as at Stalag 7-B. You could hear the guards patrolling the halls constantly.

On what I think was the second day, the interrogating officer paid me a visit. Speaking perfect "American English" and being quite friendly, he worked on me to find out the name of my unit and other details. We had, of course, been instructed to give only our name, rank and serial number. I told him that. After a time, he began to lose his composure, explaining, "If we don't know your unit, then how can we know that you are not an espionage agent? You parachuted out of the sky so we don't know where you came from unless you identify your unit. If you don't tell me you won't have Prisoner of War status. The Gestapo will take you and shoot you as a spy."

I didn't know any real important information but I knew that if I did something wrong, however unwittingly, I could endanger other flyers. I was plenty worried but I thought he was bluffing. When he kept pushing and threatening I finally told him he'd better treat me good because we had the war almost won and soon I might be interrogating him! He really got angry and stormed out saying the next people I saw would be the Gestapo.

The next day, to my relief, they took me (and a B-26

gunner) to join 61 other Allied flyers in a little rest home hospital in the mountains nearby, and marched the rest off to Nuremburg. From there we watched our P-47's dive-bomb Frankfurt and heard the artillery and tank battles. One day - March 29th - five jeeps loaded mostly with war correspondents liberated us with no opposition from the Germans. The first group to be liberated in the war.

Remembering how joyful I was, even after only 22 days in captivity, I have always had great respect and appreciation for those in WWII, Korea, and Vietnam who *really* withstood some terrible ordeals in POW camps.

I was hospitalized for a time and then shipped home on May 8 — the day Germany surrendered. Florence and I were married. We were high school sweethearts and she had waited for me. After a glorious 60 days at home I reported to Luke Field, Arizona, near Phoenix, on V-J day, the day the Japanese surrendered. I applied for a regular commission in an operational jet fighter outfit, but it so happened that 10,000 other pilots wanted to do the same thing so I didn't get the chance. Instead, they made me an instructor, teaching Brazilian students how to fly an AT-6 at Luke.

I was saved from that by an emergency leave when my father passed away on December 16, 1945. My dad was a great influence on my life, and his passing at the young age of 48 was a great loss to mother, my sister, four brothers, and myself. He lived a very productive life and raised a good family. He was rather quiet but he was always first to help other people in distress. He had great dignity and was respected by all who knew him. He was the best living ex ample of integrity I ever knew. I feel I will be real successful in my life if there are half as many sincere words of commendation and praise for me at my passing as my father had. He and my mother both came from a hardy pioneer tradition and they certainly were true to it in every sense.

Although I loved flying, I knew that the peacetime Air Corps would be much different. I, like many others, believed we had just won the war that was to end all wars so I put in for discharge. I had gladly done my part. I knew how fortunate I was to get home with nothing worse than a stiff knee. I was just another kid involved in doing a job that had to be done, one of millions of several sides. I lived and survived. Those of us who went through WWII, Korea and Vietnam know what that means. War has a way of maturing you in a hurry and that's not all bad.

CHAPTER TWO

"Ina, I just saw the damndest thing — they're giving money away!"

I had no trouble adjusting to civilian life. The day I got out started a new chapter and I was anxious to get on with it.

Until I left for college and enlisted in the Air Corps my world was the little towns of Mt. Home and later Mt. Emmons in Northern Utah, a rough, hilly country with patches of farms cut out of the wasteland. There were several towns in the area, each with 50 to 100 families, most of them living on nearby farms and ranches. Mt. Home had one general store, a post office which was one room of a log house in which the postmaster's family lived, a red brick school house for all grades up to high school, and the Church House.

Most of the land was suitable only for pasture and feed crops. The climate was dry, our main means of support was livestock. However, we did have irrigation from water caught behind Moon Lake Dam in the Uintah mountains and we grew alfalfa, grass hay, wheat, barley, oats, corn and garden vegetables during a short season in the high altitude of 6,000 feet.

We lived two miles south of Mt. Home until 1936 on land settled by my paternal grandfather; mother, dad, five boys (I was the youngest) and our sister, Jean. We were a closely-knit family, worked hard, never had much money. It was a big treat to get 25 cents each to spend at the 4th of July celebration.

Today, we would be considered "poor," being without electricity until later, or indoor plumbing, but we made a good life off a fairly meager land. We raised and butchered our own meat, grew our vegetables, canned fruit and meat for winter, and ate the grain from our fields. (We would take grain to the mill for grinding into flour and trade the miller so many sacks in payment.)

Mother made some of our clothes, but we did buy some things. I remember it was a big occasion when a J. C. Penney store opened in the town of Roosevelt, some 30 miles southeast. We could buy work shoes there for $1.19 a pair and jeans for about $2.00. Otherwise, our luxuries were an RCA Victrola that you wound up with a hand crank and a battery radio that got all three Salt Lake stations. We got the *Deseret News* delivered by mail, about two days late. I remember I couldn't wait until Tuesday for the Sunday paper to come so I could read Buck Rogers in the comics. The first car I remember was an open, cloth-topped 1926 Chevrolet. It was quite a day when Dad bought a new 1928 Chevy from Axel Pierson in Duchesne, the first model with rollup glass windows in our area.

What we really had was each other, our pride and our freedom. These were simple but happy times. The only government we knew was the County with the law kept by the sheriff and most legal matters taken care of at the county court house. Taxes were light, mostly on property, for schools and services, and no one seemed to mind paying them. Otherwise, community activities centered around the Church of Jesus Christ of Latter Day Saints or the school. In this way we were able to have a good life, first as families, then as communities.

Let me dwell a bit on the church and the community. Functionally, our community was based on voluntary participation. None of the "officials" (let's call them that) were paid. People just gave something of their time and resources. When something had to be done or someone needed something, the entire resource of the community would be behind them.

Our first responsibility was to take care of ourselves and immediate family. If we couldn't handle that ourselves then we called on our family. And if our needs were greater than the family could handle, then we went to the church.

All who needed help from the church were given work to do. They did what they were able and got what they needed. In other words, there was never a dole but the chance to earn rightfully which is so important to the maintenance of individual freedom and dignity.

Of course, this was all based on religious faith. There is a religious foundation to all ideas of governance that rise above tyranny. In the case of the Mormon faith, doctrine centers around the family. The marriage is both for time and eternity providing it is done in the Temple by those given the sealing authority. Our life here is to accomplish the establishment of the eternal unit of God's Kingdom which is the family. If we live our lives according to the Commandments of God we will go back into God's

Presence as family units and grow and progress throughout eternity in kingdoms of our own within God's Kingdom which encompasses the universe.

This, in part, explains the reason the Mormon Church does not want the members on government relief of any kind.

Dad kept the family and farm organized, a disciplinarian without being harsh. He never hit us but we did everything he asked. Above all, he treated Mother with the greatest love and respect. I never heard an unkind word between them.

Our pride was in our farm and our work. For this Dad was looked up to and respected in the community. We had the finest Holstein dairy cows in the area and I took special pride in showing those at the county fairs.

When the other kids were swimming or doing something else, we were working longer, plowing deeper; we would disc our land and harrow it. We'd make a fine seed bed and spend a lot more time on it, working our heads off before the first watering. And we would have the best crops with a higher yield.

That was Dad. He taught us to enjoy work and to enjoy the fruits of our work. We lived and ate well, never having much money, earning everything that we had, even during the Great Depression. He wasn't what you would call a literate man although he could read and was good with figures and was an excellent organizer, knew how to get things done. It was unfortunate that when he was a boy his father had needed him on the freight road when he should have been in school.

Mother was a perfect mate. She had a good eighth grade education. She had beautiful handwriting and was good in arithmetic so she wrote the letters and kept the farm books.

She was a fantastic cook, using the old wood burning stove. She bottled fruit and vegetables all summer so our cellar was always well stocked. She made bread so good that only my wife Florence can match.

She sewed, mended, read us books and stories and made our humble home a happy place to live. She was the most unselfish person I have ever known.

Even today, I find little things coming up in my life that Mother taught us as kids.

These were hard times, the Depression years, but in our families and communities we were still able to work and produce and help each other. That seemed to be the key, to keep working and producing and surviving in spite of what was happening in the rest of the country. For us, it wasn't that rough. Meanwhile, the new federal agencies of the Roosevelt Administration had moved into town to "help" people who didn't have much to begin with and still didn't have much except the means to make a living.

One day, Dad came home from town. He was shocked and amazed.

"Ina," he said to Mother. "I've just seen the damndest

thing. *They're giving money away!"*

To Dad, which is why I had to preface my remarks to keep things in context, money was *real* and represented toil and sweat. Money was a commodity, like milk or wheat or beef. It represented *useful things.*

Now how can I state what I want to say any more emphatically? *"They're giving money away!"* To Dad that was incomprehensible. He understood helping others with his own substance but he never understood the government giving something for nothing. I heard him lecture my uncle about there being "no free lunch." He taught us that we do pay for everything we get — if in no other way it will be in loss of character.

I don't specifically recall much talk of politics at home, although Dad didn't like what Roosevelt's policies were doing to change people. He couldn't understand people who wouldn't work because the government paid them relief if they didn't work. I'm sure he recognized that in some urban areas there wasn't any work, but in our farming area there was always ample food and work available. He felt that the government dole to those people was primarily used as an excuse to use government money to buy votes which corrupted the people as well as the office holders.

CHAPTER THREE

"Let's Have Lunch..."

After getting out of the service I was as politically naive as any other kid who grew up while fighting the war. I had no idea that something had been shaped in me. There was peacetime work to do, a living to make, a family to grow. There was no time or need for social philosophy.

Fresh out of the service, I didn't have enough money to get into farming as I would have liked so I went to work for an Arizona insurance company. I soon became district manager of a territory in northern Utah. We sold a lot of insurance, and made good money for those days. The only trouble was that the state manager was keeping commissions that didn't belong to him, but to the salesmen. Still naive, I tried to lead a revolt of the district managers. How could they allow themselves to be put upon like this? Well, I found out. To my surprise, they didn't have the courage to stand up for themselves and left me standing alone. I couldn't work for a man I didn't trust, so I resigned my position as district manager and returned to Arizona. Here I found out that the company didn't care, either, so I wanted no part of that kind of operation.

I decided to go back to school. I'd had an agricultural scholarship at Utah State but my days of farming were over unless I could make enough money to buy a farm. Working and with the G.I. Bill making just enough to keep us going, I went to Arizona State and majored in Business

Management and Economics. I studied for two years and
came within 16 credit hours of the degree when the opportunity I was looking for came along.

To support us I had started working part-time for a car
dealer in Phoenix. I found I liked selling cars. Cars were
solid things that people needed and wanted, things that
were real. It was a business in which you could be honest,
offer fair value, if you really wanted to, and work at giving
people a good deal. Operating that way, they would trust
you, send friends and relatives to you, and you would be
successful. I sold Dodge-Plymouth for Ed Spear and later
went into a small used car business on East Van Buren with
Dean Wyant. Then I got the chance at a Pontiac franchise
in Ajo. Dean didn't want any part of it and told everyone
on the street I'd be "broke" in 90 days. I proved him
wrong.

That was in the summer of 1950 and the start of a very
gratifying period of our lives. Ajo is a small community,
built around a copper mine and smelter, with a strong
Hispanic population. Great people, hard working, and
with a healthy outlook on life — just a pleasure to be with.
Having this kind of relationship, we made the dealership
prosper in four years. A local joke was that the Pontiac
was "the Mexican Cadillac." There was no slur intended
and no one seemed to mind.

In 1952 I took my first active part in an election.
Howard Pyle won re-election as Governor. My old flying
friend, Barry Goldwater, became a Senator when
Eisenhower won in a landslide — but not in Ajo where we
Republicans were outnumbered about 8 to 1.

In 1954 Pontiac was ready to put a new dealership in Glendale. That was a plum and a lot of people had more money than I did to buy it but I had established a record in Ajo of selling the highest percentage of Pontiacs in the total market (26 percent) and I got the dealership.

I watched politics from that new vantage point. New issues began to develop in my mind; constituencies were beginning to develop from the new business.

The gubernatorial race of 1958 was interesting and a real breakthrough for Republicans in Arizona. The Phoenix newspapers claimed that the Democratic nominee, Attorney General Robert Morrison, had abandoned a wife and child in the San Francisco Bay area, floated some bad checks, and was generally considered a scoundrel. Before the expose he should have been a shoo-in for governor. He wasn't. The Republican, Paul Fannin, won.

Whether Morrison was treated unfairly or not I didn't know, but I was delighted that the Democratic Party stranglehold on the state government was broken because there were a few things I wanted to see done in the state that that party failed to do.

The major one was tax equalization. Our property tax structure was a real shambles. All property was supposed to be assessed at the full cash value but it wasn't, instead being arbitrary to the point of just inviting abuse. New economy homes in the modest income areas were being assessed at 35 percent of their value and older, expensive, homes were assessed at five to 10 percent of value. Commercial property was assessed at from 2 percent to 10 percent. Who owned the property and where it was located seemed to make the big difference. I wanted to see this inequity straightened out.

Another problem was state spending which was growing faster than the economy and the population. We were emulating the federal government and compounding a tax problem that was getting out of hand, working hand-in-glove with the federal bureaucracy to give up more and more state and local authority to the federal government.

I was beginning to see something working in the society that I did not want to see: *purposeful sabotage of people, economy and social structure.* This is "heavy stuff," as the kids say these days, but I was beginning to get the feel, the uneasy feeling for what was going on. To wit, to prove that the free economy doesn't work, you help to destroy it. I will deal with this in a following chapter centered on the methodical destruction of the automotive industry in the United States.

But on to lighter things. I'd had talks with Bill Pyper who had been a state senator in 1952-53 about the state legislature and politics in general and he told me how to get on the ticket, how to run. Paul Fannin was up there alone with a hostile Democratic legislature and he needed me. I was going to run.

I called the county chairman to ask for nominating petitions. "Let's have lunch," he said.

So I show up for the lunch and there are a half-dozen guys there.

"We don't need you to run." I was told. "We've already got a candidate."

"Well, now, Ev," someone else said. "What else did you want to talk about?"

I replied that I didn't want to talk about anything else in particular, that I had some issues in mind and felt like running on behalf of those issues and what did they have in mind besides asking me to back off?

They told me the name of their candidate, Ralph Burgbacher. He was a wealthy man and was willing to run. "There are two slots," I said. "Get him in and help me get in. We'll probably make a good team."

I was told that I didn't understand. "Why don't you run for the house seat from your district?" I replied that Bill Barkley was my representative and that he was doing a good job.

"But he is a Democrat," I was told. I just shrugged at that. Bill was a very good man.

"Why don't you be a county supervisor?" was the next offer. I said it so happened I didn't want or need to be a county supervisor. And so the talk went on.

By the time I got back to my office at the dealership I was more mad than disgusted. I got on the phone to those who had urged me to run and explained what had happened. By the third call I had enough affirmative answers to where I could tell the county headquarters to circulate my petitions.

Burbacher and I both ran. The Democrats were Frank Murphy and Joe Haldiman Jr. Haldiman received the most votes and I came in second to fill the other spot.

I took my seat in the State Senate in January, 1961. I didn't have anyone to fill me in about the senate, but I'm a good observer and it didn't take long to learn the ropes. I was one of four Republicans in a 28 senator body. Inasmuch as there was no one running against Clarence Carpenter for President, Harold Giss for Majority Leader, and Robert Prochnow as Chairman of the all-powerful Appropriations Committee, they were again installed as the "Leadership."

Their election was assured by the fact that 19 of the 28 Senators were totally controlled by the downtown power brokers or Establishment as they are usually called now. In 1960 the State of Arizona was controlled through the leadership of the State Senate. Frank Snell, a prominent lawyer and Chairman of the Board of Arizona Public Service Company was the central figure who exercised control. His law firm, Snell & Wilmer, represented many of the largest economic interests in Arizona. The rest were represented by Jennings, Salmon, & Trask who coordinated their support with Snell. Add the influence of the Bimson family through the Valley National Bank and Publisher Eugene Pulliam and his *Arizona Republic* and *Phoenix Gazette* and it made running the state quite a neat and easy assignment for the Senate!

Nothing of real importance went through without the

approval sign being given. I noted quite early that very few of the Senators carried the big loose-leaf notebooks of the bills under consideration to the committee meetings for reference in committee work. Instead, most of them had a small loose-leaf with a summary of the bills written for easy reference. They were written up so the Senator knew how to vote and why. When I saw the write-up on my Tax Equalization bill I could see that whoever wrote the instructions didn't want equalization but preferred the *status quo*. I worked for those two years and could get only enough support to get the bill passed out of one committee in each year. No one had a better idea. Everyone professed to want a tax equalization program fair to all but very quietly everyone knew that it would not be seriously considered for a long time.

I did have a few successes to justify my $1,800 per year. We resurrected a Time Sales Finance Disclosure Act that had lain dormant for years in the Senate without action. It was designed by the Arizona Auto Dealers Association to protect the public against dishonest auto financing tactics of some car dealers and finance companies. I got Charlie Goff, a retired Chevrolet dealer, to help and we convinced other Senators that we really wanted to protect the public against the few unscrupulous dealers and we got it through long before the federal government got into the act.

I tied a tough narcotics code we needed badly onto a bill to outlaw the Communist Party, along with a loyalty oath for public officials that had a lot of public pressures for passage and tried a maneuver that Giss's ego helped me work. He had stalled the bills for 28 days in Judiciary Committee. I told the Senate President I would make a motion to bypass the committees and report the three bills to the floor for the whole Senate action. You can work this only if you can get the votes and I doubted that I could get them but it was my only chance. Giss took the bait and finally, after heated discussions, brought them out rather than face the possibility that he couldn't hold his majority votes together in opposition to bills with so much public pressure for passage.

With that narcotics law Arizona went from having the weakest of drug laws to one of the strongest narcotic codes among the states.

I always went along on everything that I could that didn't violate my principles. If I voted against a bill I didn't make a fuss about it but when I did really have to oppose something as being wrong, I expressed my reasons and was sure to make my point. As a result I built many good friendships and got along well with almost everyone.

That paid off one day when Giss had a pet deal to spend $65,000 tax money on a TV show subsidy that was not justified. He tried to ram it through in one day and I was able to put an amendment on it on the floor that had the effect of killing it. He was afraid the power structure was losing control so all business was suspended for three days while they replaced committee chairmen they thought were getting too friendly to Sam Steiger, my Republican fellow-maverick from Prescott, and myself with others who pledged complete loyalty.

The most amusing case of all was the manner in which some liquor legislation was passed. In the Special Session of 1961 to reform the liquor laws, I was surprised when Senator Wine from Pima asked me to find out what the Governor "would settle for." This indicated that The Establishment wasn't in agreement and had not sent out The Orders so Steiger and I went over to talk to Governor Fannin. We apprised him of the situation and suggested that he was in a position to get what he wanted in the bill because the pressure was on the Democrats. He was hesitant to do it and would not tell us what he wanted or would settle for. I called him at the end of the day and again the next morning and urged him with the same results. Our last words weren't very friendly.

When I walked into the Senate chambers, Wine was waiting for a report from me. I agreed I had seen the Governor — but surely he didn't expect me to report to him what the Governor had said! He told me to quit playing games because it was serious. He wanted the Governor's answer. I told him I wouldn't give it to him directly but if I was on the Conference Committee, I would suggest the following provisions on the reform bill. I gave them to him in order. He assumed I was passing along the Governor's wishes — that was exactly how the bill came out for the final vote.

I voted against a lot of spending bills because we were wasting money. It was taking over $250 million to run the state. How little I knew then. In 1981 we were spending over $2 billion and wasting more than the old budgets had been.

CHAPTER FOUR

Playing Hardball with the Big Kids

In 1962 I got into the "big league" of politics almost by accident. In the State Senate I learned that one's ability to accomplish things was not so much your own vote as it was your ability to get others together, convince them, and get them to get things done.

I had become fairly well-known because of publicity on some key issues I had pushed. Apparently it was quite a novelty to have someone besides the controlled leadership making something happen.

The 1962 election was approaching and the seat in the U.S. Senate occupied by elderly Senator Carl Hayden was up for challenge, but that may be the wrong term because Hayden had not been challenged for decades. He had started as Arizona's Congressman when the state was admitted into the Union in 1912. He moved over to the Senate and had been there ever since; the longest tenure in the history of the Union. The Republicans always had some sacrificial lamb on the ballot against him but no money was furnished and no real campaign was ever mounted against Hayden. As the ranking Democrat in the Senate, he headed the Appropriations Committee which adhered to the successful political dictum that "to get along you have to go along."

In the early fall of 1961 a big fund-raiser dinner for him

was announced and it was being hailed as a big bi-partisan event. President Kennedy was to be the main speaker and other notables from Washington were to be in attendance.

I was not alone in my disappointment that no Republican leaders challenged the bi-partisan "hype" for the affair. No one I contacted, including State GOP Chairman Steve Shadegg paid any attention to me. I was still so naive I didn't realize that deals were made and why Hayden always got a free ride. Many Republicans at the grassroots, however, felt that Hayden should be opposed and I joined them, particularly the Young Republicans, in trying to find a candidate.

I was sure that we could have a Republican candidate to oppose Hayden and just couldn't see this so-called bi-partisan billing of the affair go unchallenged. Failing to arouse anyone else, I contacted the chairman of the event, KOOL-TV and Radio Owner Tom Chauncey, and told him of my objections, that I was sending him a letter to this effect and was releasing a copy to the press. We were friendly and he understood my position and didn't disagree with my stand. That created quite a stir and a lot of people contacted me to say they felt the same way and wanted to help.

The State Young Republican convention, where I was a speaker, passed a resolution of support for a strong challenge to Hayden and the move gathered support, but we had no success in finding a candidate. More and more people kept telling me I should do it since the challenge was my idea, but I was far from ready for such a major move. It did get me thinking, though. My old flying friend from the Arizona Air National Guard days, Barry Goldwater, was in his second term in the U.S. Senate. He was quite a national figure and recognized as the head of the party in Arizona. When he came home in December I talked with him and he thought my running was a good idea and offered a lot of help, including raising money. That made up my mind. I got an organization together and announced for the Republican nomination for the U.S. Senate in late December 1961.

This started a political education I could never get in college. Although I had liked history and political science, I knew that a business education was far more practical. The political science classes were far too "sugar-coated" to really give anyone a preview of the real thing. I found that there were a lot of things I did not like about politics. The back-biting, jealousy, hypocrisy, and self-serving actions in politics will destroy all but the strongest and the most determined public-minded people. I have made the statement that politics badly bruises or completely destroys more than 90 percent of the people who actively participate in it. All too many fall for the slogan, "You've got to go along to get along."

I like people. I enjoy being a team player as long as the rules meet acceptable standards. I strongly dislike bickering and controversy, but I dislike unfairness even more. When faced with things that are not right I have found that I prefer to fight rather than settle for the wrong things being done. I remember in grade school when some of the other kids got to forming a small gang to push some of the rest of us around. I put up with their bullying for a few days and was so miserable that I decided a good licking was preferable so I took on the kid named Bud Olsen that was bothering me the most. He was one year older than me but not much bigger. I was scared to death he would half kill me when I took to him. I found, to my surprise, that he wasn't half as tough as he talked. We didn't do any more damage than bloody noses and he was just as ready to quit as I was. Afterward we became very good friends. It taught me that living in misery under intimidation just isn't necessary.

My real-life political education didn't bring a lot of tests, but the ones I did have made me wonder why so many people feel they have to go along with wrong actions. It had just the opposite effect on me. I don't take any personal credit for that. I believe I was born and raised that way and would have had a hard time trying to do anything else.

In the period after announcing that I was going to run for the United States Senate came one test. A man named George Fowler called me on the phone, addressing me as Senator and told me he had done a lot of work for Goldwater and would like to help me. He said he had been a railroad detective before he retired and his work was mostly behind the scenes; he would help me in the same way. I hardly knew what to make of this so I listened but said very little.

During December of '61 and January of '62 he would call me quite often and give me tidbits of information and then ask me questions. I really didn't think I would have need for any "behind the scenes" work so I continued to listen but say little.

One day George called and said that I was going to be contacted by a representative of the downtown Establishment he referred to as "they." "They" did not want me in the Senate race against Hayden. "They" didn't think I could beat him but "they" didn't want to take any chances so "they" were going to offer me an alternative. I would be given plenty of money to run for re-election to the State Senate, he said, hinting that there would be more for other purposes if I needed it. I would be given a lot of publicity; I would be co-sponsoring all the right bills; I would be making lots of speeches and representing the Governor often and get a real good two-year build up. Then, in 1964, Governor Fannin was not going to seek re-election and I would be the heir-apparent. "They" would then support me with publicity, money, and influence to be Governor in 1964 and I would go in easy as pie. It sounded so preposterous that I hardly gave it a second thought.

In a few days, George called again and asked if I had been contacted about the downtown deal. I hadn't so he repeated what I was to be offered again in great detail. This time it started to dawn on me that I was actually being propositioned. I discussed it with Sam Steiger and we both felt if it was a proposition that it would come again. It did, just a few days later. George came to see me in person and carefully repeated everything he had said on the phone. A man would contact me with the offer from the mysterious downtown "They." If I showed any interest I would then be invited to talk directly with the big people to make the deal. By this time I knew they could deliver everything he was offering. It both frightened me and made me angry to think that someone would think I could be bought like this so I really unloaded on George. I felt sure that he was that contact man and was testing me to see if the invitation should be made. I didn't let him know that I had him figured out but told him I would never deal with any such den of thieves. I said that I may never hold any high political office but if I ever did it would not be the result of any "deals." He got the message.

George called on me some years later in my newspaper office. He was furious at his former employers. I kidded him a little, telling him I had known he was actually the "contact man" he said would come to see me in 1962 to get me out of the Senate race. He grinned and asked me how I knew. When I told him it didn't take too much to put two and two together, he admitted it. He dictated a statement to my secretary and signed it and gave it to me in case I ever wanted verification in the future.

We came close to pulling the upset of the decade, but close doesn't count in politics. Senator Hayden won re-election by the closest margin in his life and they really pulled out all of the stops to do it.

Before securing the nomination, though, I had a strong and bitter challenge from Steve Shadegg. He had gained a national reputation as Barry Goldwater's campaign manager, and had previously run some Democrat campaigns, including Senator Hayden's. He had been installed as State Chairman by Barry. I didn't talk to Steve before announcing my intentions to run because I felt that clearing with Barry was sufficient. After announcing, I had a conversation with Shadegg, in the company of Sam Steiger. He brought up the subject of the Senate race and warned me that I wasn't going to get a free ride. He said I would have an opponent, and it might be him. I guess this was supposed to scare me out of my skin. It had the opposite effect.

Steve's account of that race as written in his book *What Happened to Goldwater* and mine are worlds apart, just as our campaign tactics were worlds apart. He blames his defeat to me on the fact that Goldwater asked him to run against me but publicly stayed neutral as the "correct" thing to do. He professes that he got into the race because of my tactics which were hurting the whole party, yet he announced in March while I was busy in the State Senate, spending only a little time in early organization. He claims that he tried to explain the "subtleties of the problem" to me and get me to not take any action until the whole party was in agreement but that I refused to listen. No such conversation took place, that I can recall. I can only assume that Steve's recollection of the facts were tainted with an inclination to record a justification for the loss that would make him look good and me bad to posterity. The details are not germane to our subject here except for the lessons in politics.

Early in the campaign I read a manuscript that my campaign manager, Mac Matheson, had on how to win elections. He said Shadegg had been paid to write it for the U.S. Senate Campaign Committee. Later Shadegg published it in hardback. The gist was that you research your opponent and get everything you can on him and plan to bring it out at the worst time possible. In your own case, if you have anything that your opponent can have on you, bring it out yourself early so it can be to your least disadvantage and he can't surprise you with it. No place did I find the issues suggested as the real basis that I felt should guide a campaign. I had nothing to fear from Shadegg's research on me and I ran the campaign on the issues and ignored his attacks on me.

"Party unity" was another phrase I learned had a new meaning in 1962. Shadegg was always proclaiming that he would support the winner of the Republican Primary in the general election. I responded to this question with some qualification. I pointed out that my word was not given lightly and if given it was binding on me. I couldn't see how Shadegg could attack me so viciously and be so sure he could support me in the general. Apparently he was sure he was going to win and wouldn't have to make good on his word; on the other hand I felt confident of victory and didn't think that problem would ever face me.

As it was, I won a comfortable victory. Shadegg was bitter. The "party unity" pledge vanished. Instead of joining as a unified slate in the general election I was informed that we would each run our own race. I was hardly welcome at the state headquarters and the new state chairman, Dick Kliendienst was overheard in a conversation by a friend of mine telling a TV broadcaster that they were quietly working for Hayden. I received less than $10,000 in financial help from the party and the promise from Goldwater that he could raise $50,000 for me from out of state sources turned out to be a belated $5,000. I was gaining rapidly toward the end of the campaign and appealed to Victor Johnson, director of the Senate Campaign Committee of which Goldwater was the Chairman. I needed just a little help to offset the barrage of newspaper, television, and radio ads for Hayden by members of the Senate telling the people of Arizona how important it was to keep Hayden in office. I never got the help.

After the dust settled on the 1962 campaign I totalled it up as a great experience. As a bunch of neophytes we had made them bring out the best and most expensive "Madison Avenue" type campaign in the history of the state to beat us. Even with that, our enthusiastic grassroots organization would have prevailed had The Establishment not used the weapon of fear that if Hayden wasn't re-elected Arizona would never get the Central Arizona Project through Congress. There is a great irony there that I will tell later on the real story of water and that project. In 1982 we still don't have CAP water but hope springs eternal, just like politician's promises.

What I really developed in the '62 campaign was a love and appreciation for the great people of Arizona. I covered every nook and corner of the state. I shook at least 50,000 hands and worked myself into exhaustion but I really learned what made the heart of Arizona beat. This made the campaign worth all the heartache and effort.

CHAPTER FIVE

1964 - 1974
The Transition Years of Leaderless Drift

The fourteen years between 1960 and 1974 were very damaging years to America. In retrospect it is easy to see that they were wasted, drifting years when we just couldn't seem to wake up from a long nightmare.

In 1960 John F. Kennedy beat Nixon in a race so close that it took late returns from Illinois to swing it to Kennedy. Some even gave Mayor Daley of Chicago credit for exhuming some extra "tombstone votes" to turn the tide.

There were no clearly cut issues or differences between the candidates on which voters could make their decisions. They finally had at it about whether Quemoy and Matsu, two little islands off the China coast, belonged to Red China or Nationalist China, possibly out of desperation to have a subject to debate. The affair was televised. Nixon looked like he needed a shave. The Kennedy charm won.

Under President Kennedy, the nation went further adrift. With a few exceptions, there was no strong direction from national or state leadership. States, counties, and cities as a whole joined minorities and pressure groups in rushing to Kennedy's "Washington Camelot" to get all their problems solved with easy money from the "New Frontier" money tree. With no strong hand in control at any level it was a time of irresponsibility in the extreme.

Perhaps the greatest damage during this period was to install the welfare state as a permanent national policy. It meant that everyone who was born into the world had a right to call upon the government for a living whether they were willing to work or not. The "Entitlements" were rushed through to give each group the part of the government largess they were "entitled" to with little thought about who was going to pay the bill.

There was an anti-Americanism afoot in the land, a knocking of American products and American values as though we would have to accept foreign products and values to pay for the sins of our abundance. Kennedy brought in McNamara and his "Whiz Kids" with their PERT charts to dismantle our national defense structure so the Russians would not be nervous over our superiority. Congress had completed its objective of taking Americans to rebuild the economies of Japan and Germany. Now that they were firmly established to be our chief competitors in world markets, it was time to continue to transfer American tax dollars in even larger amounts to almost any nation who held its hand out. Not only was the government entitled to take from the "haves" and give to the "have nots" in America but that was extended to the world. Then to cover up their generosity with taxpayers' money, Congress continued to mortgage the lives of future generations by putting the government further and further in debt.

The position of constitutionalists was purposely distorted by the media and Socialist politicians and scholars. They had the power and wanted to hold it and secure complete and permanent control. Those who opposed them were branded as selfish reactionaries, wanting to turn the clock back to Neanderthal days. The Constitution was completely swept away as far as its limitations on the activities of the federal government were concerned, and the cities, counties, and states joined in with gusto. Their politicians loved the ease with which this enabled them to perpetuate themselves in office with the benefits of the "free federal money" to pay for pet projects, patronage, and sometimes larceny they couldn't justify to local taxpayers.

What I saw in the 60's and early 70's was a dangerous drift to weak government at all levels, dominated by the vast and growing bureaucracy for the purpose of supporting itself and a Congress controlled by politicians bent on re-election through rampant spending. In areas of spending and just plain meddling, the national establishment constituted too much government; in legitimate concerns, facing the tough questions, federal government was weak, cumbersome and incapable of effective administration.

In 1964 Goldwater's nomination proved that there was a lot of strength building against the liberal excesses. I was at the convention in San Francisco when he was nominated and felt the mood of the delegates. The liberal cabal of Rockefeller, Scranton, and company didn't even have a chance. There was little need of convention strategy. The majority of the delegates simply represented the feeling across the land that Republicans were tired of nominating me-too leaders who did not represent any change in direction from the Democrat Socialism started by Roosevelt and followed in general by every administration since, regardless of party. Goldwater was the only national spokesman they had and he had their total support.

Goldwater's acceptance speech was magnificent and made me have some confidence that he would really take the campaign to the people on the basic principles and issues. The press and the Eastern Liberal Establishment would do their best to cut him to ribbons because if he won they would lose their control; so it was allout war. His only chance was to go directly to the people in person and on television.

Goldwater's campaign never got off the ground. He went to Hershey, Pennsylvania to meet with Eisenhower, Scranton, and others who had opposed his nomination and criticized his acceptance speech. Apparently, he reached an accommodation. Many of his own people seemed to be shunted aside and those representing his former opponents appeared to take over. The only real straight-talking speech with any guts in it was the acceptance speech. I waited with great anticipation for him to get hot and he never did.

He may not have been able to beat Lyndon Johnson anyway. There was a sympathy for Johnson that seemed to say he should be given a term of his own after becoming President upon the assassination of President Kennedy. Time and tide of emotion were on his side but the historic failure of the New Deal, Fair Deal, and New Frontier should have been against him. These issues begged for an articulate challenge and it never came in '64. Barry was put on the defensive and never got on the positive track.

After the election the party was handed back to the Eastern liberals which the press gleefully proclaimed as a complete rout of the conservative forces. They announced the death of conservatism forever and had it not been a strong and viable force they would have been correct. One indicator of the strength of the conservative movement was the amount of money Goldwater raised in small donations with television appeals. The big money and control politicians were with Johnson but a lot of small donations to Goldwater probably set a record for any Presidential candidate.

As President, Lyndon Johnson was far more effective in pushing America farther and faster into socialistic welfare statism than Kennedy. Although the government was getting almost completely out of control, he did exercise a lot of control with Congress to push things faster and further from any hope of containment of federal power.

Lest I be charged with making "sweeping generalizations," I am not condemning every act of those many administrations from Roosevelt to the entrance of Reagan in 1980. There was just cause for some parts of the social legislation. The Founders of this nation didn't believe in racial discrimination and the system they set up was not tolerant of it. They did make provision for the poor and disabled who could not help themselves. They had a great desire to see the masses educated. The rights and freedom of every individual were just as important as that of any other, regardless of color, creed, education or economic station in life. I have just as much empathy for the downtrodden and disadvantaged as anyone and more than most. What I am calling attention to is that the democratic socialists have accused the Constitutional system, as set up by the Founders, as not being capable of caring for the people and that is just not true. In making this charge, they then use this as their excuse to violate the system and throw off the restrictions that the Founders put on federal government to keep it from the very excesses we saw doing so much damage to our economic, political, and social structures.

Every needed social change is provided for in the Constitution. Most of the powers usurped by the federal government from the states (which has put us in the present mess) were to be left to the states to handle where they could be done better and at less cost to the taxpayers. It is really the democratic socialists who were insensitive to the real needs of the people because they aimed everything toward materialistic man and ignored the most important attributes of a happy life, which are freedom and personal dignity. We were not born to be a number in a mindless federal computer. We were born to keep most of our government local and close to us so we could control it and make it our servant instead of our master. That was the genius of the Founders' success formula and we have allowed it to be thrown out at our peril.

Again, in 1968, there was no real opportunity for Americans to express their preference in the Presidential choice we had. Hubert Humphrey, the Democratic nominee, was such a socialistic ideologue that even a basically unpopular man, as Richard Nixon was, could be elected over him. There was no challenge to the basic direc-

tion of the national drift. The discussion was mostly sur-
face issues. Nixon made some converts with his promise to
stop federal usurpation of states' powers and return many
already taken. As could be expected he did neither but continued the concentration of power to Washington.
Ironically, Nixon was able to get many liberal-socialistic
programs through because Republican members of Congress would have properly opposed them if proposed by a
Democrat. Unfortunately, they didn't oppose increasing
Socialism under Nixon.

The total repudiation of the liberal-socialists by the
people of America was magnificently demonstrated in the
1972 election. George McGovern, one of the most
bleeding-hearted liberal-socialists of all time, captured the
Democratic nomination and was more soundly defeated by
Nixon than Goldwater was by Johnson eight years
previously. I have no desire to take anything deserved
away from Nixon but we must admit he was a basically unpopular man. Certainly he deserves some of the credit for
his victory over McGovern but the crushing defeat was
primarily a complete repudiation of all that McGovern
stood for.

During this almost leaderless drift of the 60's and early
70's I was busy trying to effect some changes on the local
scene.

Early in the spring of 1963 I was visited by two men who
introduced themselves as Bill Sitton and Willard Parsons.
Bill was the business manager and Willard the production
manager of the *Arizona Journal*. It was a daily newspaper
that was started in February of '62 by Robert Morrison.

Morrison had been so angry at Eugene Pulliam and his *Arizona Republic* and *Phoenix Gazette* for their exposes on him in the 1958 election that he got enough public-subscribed stock money to start an opposition paper.

Morrison had climbed the political ladder from Pima County Attorney to State Attorney General and in 1958 had won a bitter primary race for the Democratic nomination for Governor. The state was so predominantly Democratic then that their nomination usually meant election, but not this time. The *Republic* published things about Morrison's life in California before coming to Arizona that caused the Arizona voters to unexpectedly elect Paul Fannin, the Republican, instead.

Morrison's paper had great support at first but attacks on Pulliam and lack of competitive quality in the newspaper lost much needed support. Sitton and Parsons told me that the *Journal* was nearly broke and the Internal Revenue Service was about to padlock the doors because withholding taxes in amounts over $200,000 hadn't been paid. They wanted me to put a group together to save it.

I liked the editorial policies of the *Republic* and *Gazette* and they were good newspapers in many ways. The main trouble was that they were too dictatorial with their monopoly on print communication and often only printed one side of issues on which they had a position. A competitive newspaper seemed very desirable for the area so I agreed to look into the *Journal* proposition.

A quick check of the *Journal* books showed it might have a good chance if it were operated properly; a few of us put up $50,000 to take it over and keep it open long enough to study the situation. A close look convinced us there were far too many problems with the *Journal* but that another newspaper was feasible. Fortunately Morrison got a group of Democrats together and convinced them to come up with the money to buy us back out of the *Journal* and keep a "Democratic voice." Inasmuch as the IRS had agreed to let us pay off the tax liability in payments if we would keep it open, they did the same for him after some prodding from Senator Hayden's office. The *Journal* didn't last much longer, however, and the IRS finally took over with an even larger tax liability.

By using only half of the income the *Journal* had in the beginning, as a projected figure, it looked like a newspaper could be successful if it were run in a businesslike manner. It looked good enough for a number of us to put up the money to build a new building and put in the new offset method of printing. The *Journal* had been the first daily to use this method, which was much less costly to set up and gave much better quality printing. In fact, we purchased the presses out of the defunct *Journal* from the Hoe Press Company.

We assembled a small crew of good professionals headed by Art Heenan, former City Editor of the *Republic* as Managing Editor. The news staff included Jack Karie, Tom Rippey, Ron Van Doren, Blake Brophy, and Gene McKinney who didn't necessarily represent my political philosophy but I didn't want the news to be anything but straight down the line news anyway. I thought that if we really got the truth to the public, that they would take the necessary actions to correct the problems that kept growing in our political institutions. That was too idealistic to be the end result all the time, but we did a lot of good, and I had a whole new lifetime of experiences in the 10 years we published the *American,* as it was called.

We started our afternoon tabloid in September, 1963 and built our circulation to 27,000. We had UPI and *Chicago Tribune-New York News* wire services. The paper was lively and informative but the advertisers didn't buy. They feared what the *Republic* would do if they were seen in our paper so we never got even half the support Morrison had with the *Journal.* I found that the attitude toward competition is much different in the newspaper field than in the automobile business. In the car business we had tough competition and knew that we were just going to get a part of the business and didn't hate our competitor because he got some, too. In fact we retained a very friendly relationship with our auto dealer competitors, but not so in newspapering. Newspaper publishers seem to feel that they have a right to their monopoly and anyone who threatens competition is a sworn enemy who must be crushed, even brutalized. This is one reason many cities have only one newspaper giving the public only one point of view. It is another reason that large segments of the public are somewhat cynical, disinterested, and uninformed about government, as is reflected in our abysmal turnouts at the polls.

With the *Evening American* we had to be innovative and aggressive to try to break the *Republic's* chokehold on the advertisers so we also went to large circulation weeklies, distributed free. We set up Independent Postal Service, managed by my brother Wayne, to cover 220,000 homes to deliver circulars as well as the newspaper. We even went into several cities in Arizona with the weeklies, including Tucson. We probably could have been successful with the daily if we had been willing to be a small Westside paper but I could not see being an "also-ran" and wanted to compete head on. In 1973 we sold control to a group from out of state that appeared to have the money and expertise to take it from the break-even position of the time and really make it go.

By now I fully realized that it was impossible to cure the world's problems with news. I also found out it was much easier to criticize newspapers for not doing the job they should do than it is to do it. Having been a publisher, I have become much more tolerant of a newspaper's behavior. Publishing was an experience for me that may have been worth what it cost me and my family. It kept me tuned to the affairs of government and the world; it taught me more than could any other enterprise about people, society, the community, state, and nation.

We didn't get entirely out of the newspaper business until 1979, however, when we sold the *Tampa Neighbor* in Florida. That was a printing business and large weekly newspaper we had established there as an offshoot of the business in Arizona. Fortunately, we recovered much of the loss sustained by the *American*.

My last flirtation with politics in the 60's was an ill-fated run for Governor in 1964. Many of my supporters from '62 kept telling me I had to stay in politics and I made the mistake of running against my better judgement.

There is nothing genteel about politics. I found that the close race I had with Hayden while earning me the respect of the people as a whole, marked me as a target of most of the active politicos.

In 1964 Fannin decided he would run for Goldwater's seat in the U.S. Senate and Goldwater would run for President. Dick Kliendienst was Barry's national field director until the nomination was assured and then he came home and announced he would be the next Governor of Arizona. I was incensed by the cavalier way they decided everything by themselves but what really worried me was the disastrous effect a Kliendienst candidacy would have on the party and elections that fall. The Democrats still had a big registration edge over Republicans, which meant that we had to get a lot of Democrats to vote for Republicans in order to win. Not only did I think Dick could not appeal to the Democrats but also that he would make a poor Governor if he did win. With little preparation for that race, I announced I would run against Kliendienst for Governor.

It was a mistake from the first. We weren't organized very well; we seemed to be immobilized by the disjointed times we were in. People who weren't enthused about Dick still felt that they had to support him because if he lost in Arizona it would hurt Barry in the national race for President (Dick was running as "Barry's Boy"). We could never get a good grip on the issues. I lost to Dick in the primary and he lost to Democrat Sam Goddard in the general. For my part, I was glad just to get the election over with. Some said Dick lost because my supporters opposed him. I saw no evidence of that.

Dick's problems were of his own making then as they were to be later. I was never inclined to refer to him as "my worthy opponent," but neither was I going to be the source of any blood-letting vendettas within the party. The best testimony to that was my refusal, despite strong urging and promises of support, to run as an independent in the general. I refused to be a spoiler when I could have played that role so easily. I had run, in the first place, in a misdirected effort to hold the party together at the grassroots, yet Dick chose to blame me for his loss. With all the help he had, "all the king's horses and all the king's men" couldn't have convinced the Arizona majority he was governor material.

By 1966, Goddard was getting on poorly, even with his Democratic legislature. He looked to be a sure one-term governor. At this time I was so glad not to be involved in politics that when friends started making overtures about another run, I said emphatically I wouldn't be interested even if I was handed the nomination. I had my hands full with the car and newspaper business.

When it was rumored that I was going to run again I called a press conference and said I had no intentions to run for anything and would be glad just to help the party in any way I could. Harry Rosenzweig was then GOP State Chairman. He was so overjoyed to have me out of the way that he said he was going to have me and Kliendienst be the state co-campaign chairman for the party for the '66 election. He said he would call me as soon as he could tell me what he wanted me to do. As I write this in early 1982 I am still waiting for that call.

CHAPTER SIX

The Darkest Times

By 1974, I had been out of politics for 10 years, watching from the sidelines as America moved so deeply into Democratic Socialism that it seemed she could never turn back and would have to plunge over the brink of disaster.

For the 41 years since Franklin D. Roosevelt had taken office in 1933, four Democrats and two Republicans had presided over administrations that steadily took governing functions from state and local levels and concentrated the power in Washington. The Democrats controlled Congress for all but a few years by adhering to the "FDR era" political credo of "tax, tax - spend, spend - elect, elect — the people are too damn dumb to know the difference." These were the words of Harry Hopkins, the chief architect of the New Deal — not mine. Using the crisis atmosphere of the Great Depression as the excuse, the Roosevelt Administration succeeded in throwing aside most of the safeguards of the Constitutional system and ushered in an era of Socialism under the proclaimed slogan of giving the people a "NEW DEAL." By 1936 they had packed the Supreme Court and won a 5 to 4 decision in the Butler Case which became the landmark excuse for the destruction of Constitutional restraint. The Butler decision said in effect that Congress no longer need adhere to the Constitutional restrictions on what the federal government could do as long as its actions were for the "General

Welfare" of all the people. As if that weren't enough, the court succeeded in expanding the original intent of federal power to forbid states to erect trade and tariff barriers into the power to regulate all phases of interstate commerce, and virtual control of the economy, which is one of the basic requirements of establishing Socialist power. Their regulations in the field of freight rates have had devastating consequences. The New Deal was not new at all. The Constitutional success formula of the Founders had been literally overthrown by the age-old precepts of Socialism with modern trappings. The only new part of the "New Deal" was the use of the news media to brainwash the public to think it was new and positive. It camouflaged the old "something for nothing" carrot.

The modern "Transfer Payments" was but a new name for the old political promise to take from the "haves" and give to the "have nots." Known to the Founders by its old name of "leveling" it was Constitutionally forbidden. With the destruction of these Constitutional restraints the New Deal politicians used the device so well that it has become an accepted "buzz word" in modern political dogma. It is the main theory of those who continue to raid the public treasury and dispense public funds to buy votes to stay in office.

It was obvious that all the fault was not in Washington. The overthrow of the Constitution and resulting change of the sovereign states into vassal subdivisions of the federal superstate could not have happened unless the states helped it happen. In creating the federal government at the Constitutional Convention, the Founders' biggest concern was to make sure that the federal government could never step outside its Constitutional restraints by overpowering the states and concentrating all power in Washington. Jefferson gave voice to this fear when he said,

"Our country is too large to have all its affairs directed by a single government. Public servants at such a distance, and from the eye of their constituents, must, from circumstance of distance, be unable to administer and overlook all the details necessary for the good government of the citizens, and the same circumstance, by rendering detection impossible to their constituents, will invite the public agents to corruption, plunder, and waste. And I do verily believe, that if the principle were to prevail, of a common law being in force in the U.S., (which principle possesses the general government at once of all the powers of the State governments and reduces us to a single consolidated government) it would become the most corrupt government on the earth."

Jefferson predicted what has been happening in America. The states and local governments made the power transfer possible without the general citizenry understanding what was going on.

State and local officials, like those on the federal level, found the road to personal political success was paved with government funds. Very few could resist the lure of "free" federal money for projects for the local benefit. It was much easier to get re-elected on the basis of the amount of federal money used locally at "no cost" to the local taxpayers, than it was to stand up and denounce the destruction of basic liberties that was in process. Many political careers would be ended with a pleasant retirement before the taxpayers would come to know who really paid...and the tax, tax, spend, spend, elect, elect successes had given most politicians ample reason to believe the people were "too damn dumb to know the difference."

I had been out of the political arena since 1964 and had planned to never venture into politics again as an active participant. I didn't like the jealousies and hypocrisy I had found so much a part of the political scene. I enjoyed business and my decade in the newspaper business had almost used up my life's quota of "I must save the world" juices.

I had kept a close watch on politics, though, as a citizen/taxpayer and student of the subject and was dismayed at what was taking place. In the decade since active participation I had come to the conclusion that Washington would never change its course — short of a total collapse of our economy, which would also trigger the collapse of our political system. We were certainly on a collision course with that repeat of history from every past civilization because we appeared not to learn history's lessons. Yet one ray of hope continued to shine for me; the Constitution still existed in the hearts of the people. The legacy was still there.

My two statewide political campaigns had given me much insight into the hearts and fiber of the people of Arizona. I had been to every crossroads of the state and found they were mostly honest, hard-working, God-fearing, patriotic Americans who wanted the same things that I did for myself and my children. As long as that feeling existed in the heart of the majority there was hope.

In 1974 Governor Jack Williams was stepping out after serving two four-year terms and my thoughts kept returning to the potential of the original power of the states as the only hope to save the American Republic. The Governor of Arizona would be in position to teach, lead, and gain a consensus of the people to get Arizona's house in order and stop further federal intervention into our right of self-government in all areas retained to the state and the people by the Constitution. As a private citizen I could do very little. As Governor I could do much more. As I surveyed the potential candidates in both parties there seemed to be little likelihood that anyone but I saw things in that light.

I entered the primary and ended up second out of five candidates. The winner, Russ Williams, may have been helped by having the same name as the retiring Governor. Raul Castro beat his two opponents for the Democratic nomination and narrowly won the general election to become the first Hispanic Governor in Arizona history.

Naturally I was disappointed by the results but had every reason to believe that my ideas for the needed changes were responsible for the good showing I had made. The other four Republicans had all been in the public eye a good deal in recent years where I had not. Contributions were difficult for all candidates so there was not enough money available to run a properly financed effort and most of us were left to public appearances and the news reports to get our message to the voters. The press gave me very little opportunity for that. I could only conclude that those who did get my message were convinced. Some of the other candidates were apparently convinced because they started using my issues late in the campaign. It was most amusing to see the most liberal candidate getting a front page spread on the exact same points I had outlined one week before without publicity.

The Democrats were so fearful that Castro would not be able to win re-election in 1978 that they arranged with the new Carter administration to get him appointed Ambassador to Argentina. The appointment finally came through and Secretary of State Wesley Bolin succeeded him as Governor in late fall of 1977. Wes was rumored ready to retire and wasn't expected to contend for the nomination for a term of his own. He was a good Conservative Democrat and far more to my liking than any of the other Democrats, but Dino DeConcini, older brother of Senator Dennis DeConcini had already started putting his organization together to run for the Democratic nomination.

With the showing I had made in 1974, many people thought I could beat Dino and I looked with interest again at the Governorship. Carter's administration kept speeding up the level of federal spending and the federal government appeared to be getting more completely out of control. I was convinced that the slim hope of turning government back toward levels of fiscal and even social sanity was to organize the states to work in concerted action and force the federal government gradually back into its legal Constitutional confines.

I knew it would be a difficult task but it seemed to be the only chance we had. Washington was too far gone to ever engage in its own reform. The only path open was to get most of the states behind a small issue that the federal government was imposing on the states that raised the ire of almost all, regardless of party or of where they stood on the political spectrum. The only chance for success was a straight-forward States' Rights vs. federal confrontation. It couldn't start off with a big issue that would polarize Washington opposition. It had to be innocuous enough that the federal government wouldn't feel it important enough to start a pitched battle to stop it. It had to be a winnable issue that we could turn to rapid success and get the states starting to realize they did have some power and no longer needed to remain vassals of a federal bureaucracy. Once we had one success, the second would be easier. After a few of the small issues were won, it would start to occur to many that the federal government was out of control and the states had the power to bring it back into line, by the Constitutional Amendment route, if necessary.

I pitched "The Plan" in all my speeches and made it the center part of my campaign. We then dealt with individual issues as they related to this overall design for action.

It wasn't enough to quote the Constitution and point out that it had been systematically destroyed over the years. The federal government was spending a large part of our money in programs that would not pass the test of Constitutionality and I was not foolhardy enough to think that they would change anything just because I pointed it out. We had to have a plan of action that the public felt was rational and had a chance for success.

It wasn't hard to get people riled up over the overt actions of the federal government. The transgressions were now so all-encompassing that everyone came under dictates that were very unpopular. It was very encouraging to see audiences respond to the call to arms, so to speak, in what would be the *third revolution* in the nation's history. The first one was well known as the source of our independence from Britain. The second was so cleverly camouflaged that only the most perceptive ever recognized it happened. It was the peaceful, but effective replacement of the Constitutional operation of the federal government with the Socialist provisions of Roosevelt's New Deal. One author put it so well when he described it as the revolution that few knew had happened because it came to power singing the songs of freedom. That should not be so surprising when we see that most revolutions are started in the name of liberty and better things for the masses in order to get their support for the seizure of power. Al Smith, former Democratic Governor of New York and Democratic nominee for President in 1928, said it well though he strongly supported Roosevelt in 1932. By January 25, 1936 he had seen enough to cause him to say in an historic speech:

> *"Make a test for yourself. Just get the platform of the Democratic Party, and get the platform of the Socialist Party, and lay them down on your dining room table, side by side, and get a heavy lead pencil and scratch out the word 'Democrat' and scratch out the word 'Socialist,' and let the two platforms lay there.*
> *" Then study the record of the present Administration up to date. After you have done that, make your mind up to pick up the platform that more nearly squares with the record, and you will put your hand on the Socialist*

platform. And incidentally let me say, that it is not the first time in recorded history, that a group of men have stolen the livery of the church to do the work of the devil..."

By the early 1950's Norman Thomas, head of the Socialist Party, wrote in his book called *Democratic Socialism* "...here in America more measures once praised or denounced as socialist have been adopted than once I should have thought possible, short of a socialist victory at the polls."

In the *Congressional Record* for April 17, 1958, Norman Thomas is quoted as saying:

"The United States is making greater strides toward Socialism under Eisenhower than even under Roosevelt, particularly in the fields of Federal spending and welfare legislation."

In 1962, Thomas summed up the situation as follows:

"The difference between Democrats and Republicans is: Democrats have accepted some ideas of Socialism cheerfully, while Republicans have accepted them reluctantly."

The election of Ronald Reagan in 1980 is ample proof that the people are well aware of the failure of the Socialist plans and want to get back to sound principles in government again.

In the 1978 campaign I again had the satisfaction of seeing the basic parts of my Plan gain much favor with the voting public but again I fell short of getting the votes to gain the office where I could be effective in helping put the Plan into action.

A number of Arizona political agendas were changed in March of 1978 when Governor Bolin died after less than six months in the office. The next person in the line of succession in Arizona is the Attorney General. Rose Mofford was appointed to fill out the term as Secretary of State when he became Governor to complete Castro's term, but the succession had to go to an elected official. Since the Attorney General is next in line Bruce Babbitt became Governor. At first Babbitt said he would finish out the term but would probably run again for the office of Attorney General in the fall. His next planned step in politics was to go to the U.S. Senate when the next vacancy occurred or, barring that, when the first election for Senate came up he thought he could win. He apparently liked the political benefits of the Attorney General's office where he could profess to be the champion of all oppressed people. This is great for media coverage and it is very difficult for the public to ever get a real report card on the occupant of that office so, barring a scandal, who can dispute his claims of great things accomplished as he asks the voters in some future Senatorial election to move him on to bigger things in Washington? Bruce was known as a poor administrator to the few who knew what really went on in the AG's office and the Chief Executive job didn't really appear to be his *forte*.

Apparently, there were forces at work that quickly caused him to re-think his position and start to hedge on his political plans, maybe to seek a term of his own as

Governor? After all a man had to "play the hand that was dealt him," he said at the time, using the terminology of a gambler.

The smoldering DeConcini-Babbitt feud became public with Babbitt's change of mind. Dino held a press conference to declare that whatever Babbitt did, he was un-equivocally committed to the race for the Democratic nomination for Governor. He strongly suggested that if Babbitt was a man of his word he would be the interim Governor and run for Attorney General in the fall as he had first announced. But within a few days, Dino backed down and decided to run for Attorney General and Babbitt was given the Democratic nomination with only token op-position.

As Attorney General, Babbitt was many months, some said years, behind in performing the primary purpose of the office which is to render legal opinions to officials of state government; in areas of public relations and media publicity, however, he was light years ahead of everyone else. For reasons known only to Babbitt and the press he got far more publicity as Attorney General than any other public official in Arizona. His name identification, ac-cording to research polls was over 93 percent, a level that even Presidents of the United States seldom reach. It was obvious that regardless of the good or bad job he had done in three and one-half years as Attorney General, he had done a truly astounding job of self-promotion that made him the odds-on winner of any political contest. Pollsters had him getting as much as 72 percent of the vote for Governor against any Republican in the fall election.

I knew Bruce reasonably well and knew that he was a mainline Liberal of the Carter school. I knew how he had greatly increased the cost of operating the Attorney General's office and that most of his attention has been on publicity-seeking consumerism cases at the expense of his state official clients. I observed that he cleverly used the favorable public opinion Wes Bolin had enjoyed to make it look like he was carrying out everything Wes would have done. In reality he pushed up spending in the budget then under consideration by the legislature and quickly acted on enough key issues to convince any close observer that he would truly maintain his liberal credentials. In short, he was following the easy, time-worn, political course of buying votes.

One of the realities of politics is that the "smart money" always goes with the "best bet" especially if the candidate is pliable enough to pay a return on the investment. Babbitt had carefully set himself up as "the sure bet."

The nation was in deep trouble which was getting more serious. I had a plan that could change that course. Arizona was increasing the size of its government which resulted in a faster rate of spending than that of the federal government. Rapid growth covered up many of the problems building up because of this. Carter was already failing in Washington and Babbitt was proudly proclaiming his support of Carter and his principles. To cement that relationship Babbitt quickly appointed Carter's Carolina manager of the '76 Presidential campaign to the high-paying job as Director of the Department of Corrections in Arizona. Most all top-paying positions went to people from out of state. To prove his loyalty to the trade union leadership in Arizona, he publicly stated in an address to them in Prescott that he would put whomever they chose as labor's representative on the Governor's staff.

The list of improprieties went on and on and I felt it was long enough for many thinking people to see through Babbitt and we could raise enough money to wage a campaign that could beat him and his publicity machine. A lot of people did see through Babbitt but not enough.

The pre-sell of a landslide victory robbed me of the financial support I needed to get my story before the voters with enough impact to convince the majority. He literally shut out our fund-raising efforts in the business community. He rejected my challenge to debate but I had a telling effect and made headway in three joint television appearances. He tripped himself up on Channel 5 when he tried to use some fancy figure-shuffling to counteract my charges that he was a big spender. By very creative comparison of figures he tried to make it look like he had actually cut state spending in the annual budget. When it didn't work he got so angry as to almost lose control and even his apologist on the press corps, John Kolbe of the *Phoenix Gazette,* wrote a column calling that story of created frugality the biggest whopper in recent memory.

On the Sunday night before the election, he again got obviously angry and flustered when I handed him a copy of a report to prove he had not told the truth about having previous knowledge of a prison break that cost several lives. Had his Corrections Director acted on the information, the break may have been avoided and lives saved. At the studio, after the camera was turned off for a commercial break I reached to retrieve my copy of the report and he snatched it and tore it up and put the pieces in his pocket. Meanwhile his chief assistant stormed into the studio still with pajama tops over trousers and house slippers to demand that the station moderator restrict me from asking Babbitt questions and from allowing any rebuttal to his statements. When they refused he threatened to file a lawsuit against them.

We had planned a strong TV presentation of my issues for the six-week period before the general election. Because we couldn't raise the money for it we finally started a reduced schedule three weeks before election. Coverage by the press, although weak in my behalf, did assist in getting some of my issues out and the joint appearances plus our three weeks of paid TV and a little radio constituted our stretch campaign. We were gaining rapidly and could have closed the gap for victory had we had the funds to operate as we planned. As it was, we reduced Babbitt from his beginning of 72 percent of the vote down to a little over 52 percent. He won by just over 40,000 votes. Cutting him down to that level kept him from having any coattail effect for others on his ticket. It enabled the Republicans to gain control of the State Senate and increase our majority in the House. We regained the Attorney General's office and the open seat on the Corporation Commission in cliff-hangers. All in all it was classed by many as a moral victory for me and definitely a resounding victory for the party.

In retrospect, I had little chance to win the office but for whatever good it did the Plan had been widely-proclaimed, more finely developed, and generally accepted by the majority of the people. In a sense, I was relieved not to be into the thick of the political morass but greatly disappointed that I still had no opportunity to start to implement the program I felt was necessary before so much damage was done that even the states couldn't correct the problems in a peaceful manner.

CHAPTER SEVEN

What's Good for General Motors
Is Good for America and Vice Versa

By 1980 America was in a crisis, and in no sector of the economy was this more indicative than in the auto industry. Unfortunately, what I had been telling the public for over 20 years — the disaster I wanted to help avert through high elective office — was coming to pass. The decline of the U.S. auto industry which spearheads the economy raised the question: Was this planned destruction or the result of bureaucratic intervention?

The Industrial Revolution took its greatest leap forward with the development of assembly line manufacturing of automobiles in the U.S. The perfection of this system revolutionized the transportation industry by bringing to market automobiles at prices the general population could afford. This fired the engines of American industry, giving that nation the economic leadership of the world. Automobiles were eventually responsible for one-fourth of all jobs in the United States. As "Engine Charlie" Wilson, Eisenhower's Secretary of Defense, said, "What's good for General Motors is good for America and vice versa." This pronouncement created quite a stir but, in reality, what he said was true.

At the beginning of the decade the U.S. had a sick economy to a great extent because the country had a sick domestic auto business. It is doubtful if the industry will ever recover totally because the capital of the auto companies had deteriorated to where they may not be able to continue product improvements fast enough to meet foreign competition. The dealership organization of domestic manufacturers was weakened by the largest number of failures in the history of the business between 1979 and 1981. Interest was more than double the traditional rates and many dealers could not generate enough business to absorb these higher costs and still make a profit. Many were just hanging on, hoping for an upturn in sales early in 1982.

Many said the trouble in the car business was the greed of Detroit and its failure to react to the changing market. This is not true. Probably no industry has been as sensitive to the desires of the public as the car business. The history of the auto industry is replete with the names of companies that made cars the public wouldn't accept. Even Ford failed with the Edsel.

Without going into too much detail, here is a summary of what happened. The *labor unions* were a major factor. In the Roosevelt administration government intervened on behalf of unions to give them such control over the labor force of the industries that management was unable to resist demands for constant and inflationary increases in wages and fringe benefits. In the car business the union strategy of keeping two of the big three companies producing while striking the third made it mandatory for the struck company to give in. The result was to create a labor cost in the auto industry of more than $20 per hour in comparison to a general industrial labor cost of about $15 in the U.S. and $10 in Japan. In addition the antagonistic attitude of many labor unions caused the workers to lose pride in workmanship, resulting in American products being of inferior quality even though engineering and design were superior. Unions kept manufacturing from using new techniques and machines that would reduce labor costs for fear of reducing the number of jobs. *Government* was the other big problem. As long as free market forces were allowed to operate the people of America chose to drive big, luxurious cars. A big car can be manufactured for very little more than a small one because there is very little labor savings in making a small car instead of a large one. Fuel was cheap, but even so the big American cars were getting relatively good fuel economy.

Then in the beginning of the 70's the *environmentalists* struck. Congress was convinced that the car was the cause of pollution and must be cleaned up. They passed laws that made it mandatory for the U.S. auto makers to reinvent the automobile. While doing that, however, manufacturers had to keep making the ones already developed so they put pollution controls on cars not designed for them. The result was to reduce the economy of most cars by 35 to 40 percent. Cars with engines designed to get 16 mpg in town and 22 on the road were choked to the point that they could only do 8 to 10 in town and perhaps 13 on the road.

The price of cars went up because of the extra cost to manufacture safety and pollution equipment not included before, and the fuel efficiency plunged so the operating costs went up also. There was an increase in the sale of little, cheap foreign cars, but that was not what the American people wanted and the sale of big cars continued. Ford brought out the Pinto and Chevrolet the Vega. Neither sold well until the oil embargo in 1974 when there was a panic to small cars. Foreign cars became a premium item as did Pintos and Vegas.

U.S. manufacturers had been moving as rapidly as possible to convert their car fleets to smaller, more fuel-efficient models to comply with federal orders but that would take many years and $150 billion to accomplish. That U.S. companies weren't very far along in 1974 added to their woes because slow sales of big cars reduced profit needed to finance the changeover.

The spurt of sales in foreign cars gave other countries the capital to continue to develop their cars (Japan especially), primarily for the American market. They increased advertising, increased models, added air conditioning and power assists, improved interiors, etc. demanded by the Americans.

Another factor in the Japanese success was that the country put very little into national defense so the tax burden on Japanese manufacturers for national defense was almost nil whereas U.S. companies paid high taxes, partly to pay for Japan's defense. In addition, the Japanese home market was protected by rules and tariffs and U.S. and other "foreign" cars were almost forbidden in their market — while the U.S. maintained free trade and let Japanese cars come in with only token tariff. It was what is called "one-way-free-trade."

Technologically, the Japanese are not innovators but they are excellent copiers. They did a good job of copying

U.S. manufacturing methods and then kept improving on them. Their manufacturers had the advantage of a friendly and cooperative relationship with labor.

As a nation the Japanese know they export or perish — and they knew they had to shed their reputation for shoddy merchandise. Quality was their aim and the focus of their advertising. They improved on an American technique in manufacturing that uses computers to operate machines for operations that need more precision; the technology we call Robotics. U.S. unions slowed U.S. industry while the Japanese moved faster in this field. The use of robots was largely responsible for their cars appearing to have better quality because they had better fit of the body panels and better paint finish than U.S. models. Although the Japanese cars have never approached the life of U.S. cars overall and they have always cost much more to repair, the quality of outer fit and finish appearance coupled with heavy advertising sold the American buyers. Without proof I wouldn't accuse the Japanese of being good payoff artists, feeding the car buff magazines and some of the American press so that the attack on American-made cars reached gigantic proportions, but it makes me wonder. This reflected the attitude of the U.S. government through the 70's. "Detroit" was continually attacked in Congress and by the bureaus. The Environmental Protection Agency kept up a constant barrage on fuel economy (the public didn't realize EPA regulations had cut gas mileage 40 percent). The Department of Transportation tried to force "Detroit" to build Sherman tanks in compliance with safety regulations. All the while Volkswagens were regular firetraps, and it was the Ford Pinto that got the headlines from a few accidents where they were hit in the rear and burned. While U.S. autos were questioned publicly and constantly on safety, foreign cars killed and maimed U.S. drivers at double the frequency of American-made cars. This was never brought out.

Some feel that there was a great conspiracy to kill off the U.S. car industry in order to kill the U.S. economy. Out of the resulting economic chaos the Socialists would finish destroying the Republic and emerge with a Socialist Dictatorship in complete control and the states would become vassal subdivisions to do the bidding of the central power. Whether it was the case, events have fit the scenario.

After the oil embargo of '74 the U.S. auto industry recovered quickly. The people again chose to buy big cars and the small cars became a drug on the market. Little foreign cars and U.S.-made Pintos and Vegas went from selling at premium prices to half these prices in a matter of a few months — sometimes weeks. By government mandate, however, the downsizing of U.S. cars continued.

Foreign cars had been steadily backing up in dealer inventories and on the docks and shipments had been greatly reduced in the fall of 1978. The percentage of foreign car sales was steadily going down and there was no doubt the U.S. demand for foreign cars created by the oil embargo had run its course. As if on orders to correct this, in January of 1979 President Carter and Energy Chief Schlessinger began a barrage of public pronouncements that we were headed for an energy shortage that would bring rationing, big taxes on "gas guzzlers," and reduce our economy to a point where there would be no gas for big cars. This campaign went on for three months and by

April of 1979 the domestic car industry had headed into a big slump that continued to deepen through 1981. At this writing, January 1982, was the worst month in the history of the modern U.S. industry. In my own business, the Carter-Schlessinger show cut my Grand Prix and TransAm sales in half. It was just like a faucet had been turned off. Foreign cars turned from discounted problems and American buyers stood in line to pay well over retail sticker for those little gems. They zoomed up to 25 percent of the U.S. market from about 15 percent and by 1981 were at nearly 30 percent.

Another government action that created the scenario for this whole debacle was action in the energy market that tried to put the U.S. in the position of being forever dependent on foreign sources of oil. Without government intervention, starting back in the 60's, the U.S. oil companies were encouraged to develop foreign oil and curtail domestic sources through tax structures. So-called "environmentalists" were encouraged and given so much government help that it became impossible to build refineries in the U.S. to meet the nation's fuel requirements. It appeared that the Master Planners decided the other sure way to bring America to her knees was to make us dependent on foreign sources of energy. To help this along, nuclear energy, originally developed in the U.S., made much more progress abroad because of government, ecologists, and soft-headed judges. In addition, the environmentalists in Congress made it almost impossible to utilize our almost limitless coal reserves to help with fuel independence. And, then, the government still controlled the offshore areas where huge oil reserves exist and kept most of those areas off limits to development.

These actions were what allowed the OPEC nations to hold America hostage and start the transfer of much of the world's wealth from the industrial nations who created the wealth to people who never knew what oil was until Western technology went and developed it for them. All of this happened largely because of the actions of those who have maintained control of the U.S. government for the past 40 years and have used government to pursue their own ends. If the facts were to be published as a fiction story it wouldn't sell because it would appear too preposterous.

The United States deficit balance of payments in 1981 were entirely because of oil and automobiles. The inflation caused by government spending was pricing U.S. products out of the world market so the future looked even more bleak. Unless these trends were reversed, the only result would be a continuing decline in the American standard of living.

There was one light at the end of the tunnel for the car industry and for the whole country. Domestic manufacturers changed their cars over to smaller, fuel-efficient models. By 1982, these were superior in most ways to foreign cars in total features and value for the money. The reaction against Japanese cars was starting to be felt and their sales were dropping. Many Americans who bought foreign before were returning to American cars in 1982, the first year the U.S. had enough models on the market to do the business in small cars. While the Japanese may have been making a mistake coming out with larger and more expensive cars, they will never beat the U.S. in that field and if their bubble breaks again, as it did in 1978, there will not be U.S. government intervention to save them during the Reagan Administration. There is a good probability of foreign car sales receding to 15 percent of the U.S. market in the next five years providing the unions continue to respond to the industry demands that they get sensible on the expensive fringe benefits that now cost the U.S. makers over $8 per hour. By reducing paid vacations, excessive personal holidays (paid time off for birthdays, excessive sick leave, etc.) the cost of labor per car can be greatly reduced, thereby keeping jobs and profits in America. The auto makers had a heavy club to use on the unions in 1982 because they were telling the unions to re-negotiate these "paybacks" or car components will be made in foreign countries where labor costs are down and the U.S. industry will become assembly only. The threat is real and the unions may be responding.

Government must reduce unneeded constraints on the car industry by reducing the make-work harassment of the bureaucracies. Pollution and fuel economy have been accomplished at great costs but continuing pressures in these areas are counterproductive. Any additional improvements are at too great cost and further regulation should be relaxed. If more of the public knew it is really the consumer who pays for everything dictated by government, Congress could be forced to act more responsibly in the interest of *all* the people.

Government must make our open trade policy a two-way street. We should adopt the same trade restrictions against the Japanese that they impose on our products. It is time they also paid for their own national defense.

CHAPTER EIGHT

The Third American Revolution

If someone had told me 20 or fewer years ago that what some of us in politics were doing was fometing revolution I would have just laughed. But that's what, when you got right down to it, we were doing at this point.

While I studied and learned much about the details of government operations, developed ideas and plans for effective administration, I can say truthfully that I never wavered on basic principles. Now that the Third American Revolution is a reality, what many of us constitutionalists have worked toward all these years, I have to frown (I'm beyond outrage) on the antics of political snivelings who suddenly change sides and claim to have been with the new winners all along. While I will oppose him in the arena, I have more respect for a liberal who remains loyal to his principles and party than for someone who sways with the wind out of political expediency and believes in nothing except self-advancement. Such men, the go-along crowd-pleasers, are the ones who got us into the pickle we were in.

Historically, revolutions seem to simmer for a long time before coming to a boil. The period is somewhere around 20 years which explains partially the predominance of gray beards and bald heads in successful movements for revolutionary change. Revolutionary leadership, if it is to lead anywhere, is not kid stuff. (I had to laugh when, writing for the *Washington Post* in January, 1982, Arizona's youthful Democrat Governor wrote: "The President has once again confounded his adversaries by wading ashore on a new beachhead far beyond the battle lines. Faced with another year of trench warfare...")

The Founders were mature men led in the First Revolution by George Washington who could, indeed, talk about battle tactics with some authority; the seeds of the Second Revolution in the Roosevelt Administration were planted 30 years earlier by Socialist Eugene Debs and the administration of President Wilson. The Third Revolution began to take shape in the '50's and '60's when it was realized the temporary relief measures taken by the Roosevelt administration during the Depression were to become permanent fixtures of a national Socialism.

Some will say the use of the word "revolution" is too strong in the latter two cases because neither in the 30's nor in the 80's was power seized by force of arms. It's very gratifying that this was so and I pray that all future change in America will be without force of arms. But I don't want to let semantics dilute the realities. According to Webster's *New World Dictionary* a revolution is, among other things: "A complete cycle of events; a complete or drastic change of any kind; overthrow of a government, form of government or social system, with another taking its place."

One way to look at the variety of governance is to visualize a straight line with Total Anarchy on the right at the end of the line, Total Tyranny on the left. Under Total Tyranny there is absolute rule by a man or group issuing total ruler law. Under Total Anarchy there is no law; there is chaos.

The Founders knew their history, recognizing that neither the right nor the left was the proper government to guarantee life, liberty and the citizens' right to pursuit of happiness. Only a government that would remain in the Balanced Center — squarely in the middle along the line between the two extremes — would accomplish what was wanted, and they took great pains to write a Constitution that would establish a government of the Balanced Center and to safeguard that position.

Almost from the beginning, there was deviation back and forth along the line from the Balanced Center, but not until, beginning in 1933, was there a radical swing to the Left, to the side of tyrannical rule, and not until 1980 was there a halt to this movement and the start of a swing back to the Balanced Center. This is revolution.

The election to the U.S. Presidency of Ronald Reagan in 1980 was the first occasion in my lifetime that the people of America had an opportunity to express their wishes for a complete change in direction of government, regardless of what he may have said to the contrary. The record of President Carter before him showed he was dedicated to continue the leftward direction of government at an even faster pace than his predecessors. Mr. Reagan was the first presidential candidate in 44 years who advanced a real plan to stop the leftward direction of government and start back to the Balanced Center in orderly phases.

Ronald Reagan won by a landslide, aided politically by a crisis of grave proportions. How grave, he was soon to find out.

On taking office he found out what the Captain of the Titanic must have felt as he realized his "unsinkable" ship was really going down. The United States may not have been sunken but she sure was settling fast.

In 1982, the national debt was approaching $1 trillion, and the budget nearly $700 billion. Despite President Reagan's cost reduction program the Fiscal 1983 national budget deficit is projected to be over $100 billion. Compare that to the 1970 budget of $146 billion.

Mr. Reagan found federal spending completely out of control. Congress, over the past two decades, had built into the budget so many uncontrollable, increasing costs that the federal budget was growing more each year than the total budget was less than two decades before. Congress had not only appropriated money that wasn't there but also left open the doors of the Treasury. It is hard to understand how intelligent men and women, the cream of elected officials, could have done what they did to the American people. Mr. Reagan made the first honest, significant move in 48 years to reduce the rate of government spending increases and the first since President Kennedy to make a realistic move to reduce taxes. The only reason he was successful is because of his mandate at the polls. One thing most politicians are dedicated to is winning elections so the majority in Congress went with the winner. The old ward-heelers like Democrat Majority Leader "Tip" O'Neill were flabbergasted. They couldn't believe the people had become smart enough to see through the lies and deceit they have used so successfully for so long.

Mr. Reagan also found that he became Commander-In-Chief of a military establishment that was not as strong as Communist Russia; that while we have been actually disarming ever since the McNamara troops took over the Pentagon in 1961, the Russians have been borrowing our money, stealing our technology, buying our wheat, and getting American and other free world countries to build up their Russian industrial capacity so that they can eliminate us when they are ready. Mr. Reagan's choice had to be: build back the defense capability of America or be ready to surrender in the not-too-distant future.

He found he had become the leader of a nation that had let its government choke the free enterprise system to a point where industry is starved for operating money and profits were non-existent or too low to provide the reinvestment capital to modernize and compete. Unions have had the upper hand with power given to them by politicians milking them for votes and they pushed up the price of labor to the point where many American industries were priced right out of the market; taxes were so high that people with money were driven to spend much of their time and resources in the wasteful practice of tax avoidance instead of investing freely to make industry move and create more jobs; government regulations added an overhead burden to American industry that was intolerable. American products have to absorb the cost of America being policeman and guarantor of independence to much of the world. Our shores remain open to free trade while other nations bar our products; and the Federal Reserve Board has been wringing out the economy with managed interest rates that are the highest in modern times and are causing a hemorrhage of business failures.

This partial list of problems is why I said Mr. Reagan must have felt some kinship with the previously-mentioned ship captain.

Here I will have to reveal to you my real feelings and what I really believe or this book won't make any sense to you or anyone else. It is the reason I am sure America will survive and prosper even though our condition looked almost hopeless in early 1982.

America is not just another nation in the family of nations that have come and gone through the pages of history. It has a *manifest destiny* to lead mankind out of the darkness of ignorance, tyranny, slavery, and starvation into the glorious light of freedom, abundance, continual progress, and the joy of living that results from being free.

Almost everything about our history bears out the guiding hand of a loving God. Columbus acknowledged that it was God who inspired him to make the voyage to discover America and that moved upon him to convince his officers to sail one more day before turning back to placate crews which threatened mutiny. That was the day they sighted land.

The religious upheavals in Europe came at a time to furnish America with many thousands of hearty, God-fearing people who would brave the dangers and rigors of a forbidding wilderness in order to have religious freedom. (When Juan Peron was ruler of Argentina, he asked this question of a prominent church leader visiting his country: "President McKay, why is it that North America has prospered and progressed so much more than South America even though we too have great natural resources?" President McKay answered without hesitation, "The colonists who came to South America came in search of Gold. Those who colonized North America came in search of God!!")

The gestation period of this nation of destiny started with Jamestown in 1607 and developed step by step to the actual birth in 1776. It never happened before nor since. The process brought forth what has been acclaimed the greatest gathering of genius in the history of the world, in one place at one time, to accomplish the formation of a nation that they truly proclaimed had a manifest destiny. Almost to a man they gave God the credit.

The formation period of the nation was one continuous miracle. Meaning no disrespect for the fighting ability of the colonists, a review of that war shows the British snatching defeat out of the jaws of victory time and again. Gen. Washington certainly recognized the final America victory as Providential.

Then, to safely launch the new nation on the uncharted seas of the "first of its kind" Constitution took a lot more Providential guidance as the Founders profusely declared. Had it not been for the high caliber of that early leadership the U.S. could never have survived as a uniquely independent nation. Washington, the two Adamses, Jefferson and Monroe gave this nation a continuity of quality in leadership neither we nor any other nation has ever seen before or since.

Another Providential Leader was developing during the stormy period after the Founders passed on. Abraham Lincoln was elected, fortuitously, in 1860 as a minority President because of the split in the Democratic party. Otherwise he would not have had a chance. In service to his country he ranked with Washington in greatness by saving the Union which was destined to lead mankind to its highest achievements. He too gave credit for his success to Divine Guidance.

All too often we have elected to high office politicians who "went along to get along" but in crisis it seems that the Lord has either guided us toward exceptional leadership or perhaps caused some with questionable ability and intentions to rise to the challenge.

Today, we are in grave danger once again. Not the same kind of danger as in the beginning or the Civil War period but equally grave and much more complicated.

The measures taken by President Reagan to date will not save America. The spending cuts have only given promise to reduce the *increases* in spending, leaving unprecedented deficits in the federal budget. Rather than be able to balance the budget by 1984 the deficits were being projected as high as $100 billion per year. Yet faced with disastrous consequences and no choice but to face up to them, the large segments of the press, Members of Congress, special interests and self-serving organizations throughout the nation were viciously attacking the President for trying to bring fiscal sanity to government. It is obvious that there are many honest people misled into following the usurpers bent on total control of this nation even if it meant destroying it in the process. They were there in every age and no one should be surprised that they are present today and will always be present until the millenium.

In spite of the dark picture I have just painted, I am not discouraged. Quite the opposite. We have finally gotten so deeply into trouble that most good people, and they comprise the majority in this nation, can now recognize the source of our problems. This is the first step toward resurgence, getting back to the Balanced Center. "Come Back, America!"

The election of Ronald Reagan gave us hope that he would at least work to slow down the speed with which we were traveling in the wrong direction. Equally encouraging was the defeat at the polls of many front line Democratic Socialists who seemed to own elective office. Into the 80's we need to turn more of them out as part of the revolution back to the Balanced Center.

Mr. Reagan could not do this alone. He took some big steps in the right direction. In addition to the tax and spending cuts, he passed the word to state, county, and city officials that the federal government was going to turn back whole areas of government activities and social responsibilities. So, in addition to changing more faces in Congress, the people must vote change at the state and local levels. The federal bureaucrats did not usurp state and local prerogatives in governing all by themselves. They had plenty of help from state and local officials who found it was easy and profitable to follow the political adage of "go along to get along." The ones who have continued to push us further into our crisis cannot be entrusted to getting us out in the difficult transition ahead. The Third Revolution must put in place Governors who will see that the power to govern in all our activities, except those few powers specifically given to the federal level, are returned to the people.

We must have leaders with vision who really see the great future ahead if we unshackle ourselves, both personally and economically, from the terrible burden of too much government. We must have people in government who feel it a privilege to serve, even at some sacrifice, instead of being there for what they can get out of it for themselves. We need a great renaissance of revolutionary patriotism to root out the doom and gloom that has almost destroyed us.

This renaissance will be viewed by some and labeled by others as being negative, as turning back the clock, and turning against all the social advancements of the last 50 years. That criticism will come from those who are mired in the *status quo* and fear progress. Actually, the period ahead will bring to the people of America more and faster progress economically, technologically, and socially than ever before. It truly boggles the mind to contemplate what the people of this nation can do with the technology we have today and what that technology, coupled with the arts and social purpose, promises for the future if we can return to the free enterprise system and let it work. Our fantastic increase in knowledge, communications, and mobility unshackled man to where we can enter a new age of abundance for all. As we solve our problems in America we will emerge as the world leader in freedom and again be the example of success that awaits all nations who follow. There need be no people who are starving or even without abundance but this renewed America will be wise enough to not try to give others free help. We will merely help them to help themselves. Like the example we too often have forgotten: if you give a hungry man a fish you satisfy his hunger for the day. Teach him how to fish and he will never be hungry again! That will be the new role of America and we need no longer listen to those who want us to feel guilty for our blessings of abundance. We cannot really help others by *giving* them things. We have ample evidence to prove that point. We can do most by correcting our own problems and giving all the peoples of the world the example of the great success of our system so that they can follow as they see fit and prosper accordingly.

It won't just happen. We must make it happen. To do so we must understand the problems, why they appeared, and how to solve them.

It's time to get specific.

CHAPTER NINE

Toward the Balanced Center

I've spent a lot of time and space laying the groundwork as carefully as I could to advance ideas about returning, not to any bygone era, but to sensible government in the United States as established by the Constitution. My proposals will work. They are a composite of the best and most workable solutions I have found in my years of public life.

As I've said several times, the chief of my concerns was the drift toward Socialism as reflected in the increasing share of national income for the federal and other governments. Almost all other inefficiencies and abuses radiate from there.

For many years economists of many persuasions said that when government usurps and spends more than 25 percent of the national income we have Socialism. From 1776 to 1929 spending by government at all levels in the United States — federal, state and local combined — never exceeded 12 percent of the national income except in times of war. Two-thirds of that 12 percent was spent at the local and state levels. In 1982 government spending had reached *45 percent* of the national income, two-thirds of which was spent by the federal government!

I am talking financial sense now — not about the usurpation of powers or the creation of classes of people and other social matters. Just dollars and sense.

As quickly as possible, along a planned timetable with no footdragging, total government spending must be reduced to 25 percent of the gross national product and taxes reduced accordingly.

We found that a free nation cannot exist when such large amounts of national wealth are taken out of productivity, with an increasingly high percentage going toward the servicing of debt. The child born today is immediately in debt for $4,000 and that does not include local and state bonds.

Some will say this is not feasible, that I am talking of returning to an outdated form of government...the need to "meet the increasing complexity of society." This is nonsense. Society may be complex but it is because government has chosen to make it so, and much of the "complexity" is for its own sake and to promote and support the layering of bureaucracy.

Let me state the situation with government spending from the business standpoint. Government spending, along with personnel, grows at a highly disproportionate rate compared to economies and populations. Also disproportionately, the level of service seems to decrease. However, in almost every other enterprise involving productivity, costs and numbers of personnel required to perform a unit of work are reduced with volume. You produce a better product, provide a better service, with fewer workers and at lower cost to the consumer. The assembly line may be the best example.

In the future, the philosophy of government at all levels will have to turn around to produce more for less — to provide better service to the taxpayers at lower tax rates — by instituting management practices directed to that end. After all, this is one of the advantages of social order, working together. The purpose of society is to make life more pleasant and productive for one another.

I will be accused by bureaucratic liberals of over-simplifying the issue, advocating sabotage of social progress and advocating anarchy. This is part of their Big Lie that has been repeated so often that the people have come to accept the lies as truth. Those of us who have been intimidated in the past, let us not fear losing "Big Brother" and the false security he offers. Let's stop swallowing that old line of, "Well, if you think things are bad now, you can imagine how they would be if we hadn't started all these agencies and programs."

Two other Big Lies are associated with the distortion of constitutionalism and the New Federalism. One is that constitutional conservatives are the tools of the super-rich and powerful interests, advocating *laissez faire*. The other is that we are advocating anarchy.

Quite the contrary is true. The super-rich have become richer and more powerful during the past 50 years than at any previous time in U.S. history. These powerful interests are the ones who have controlled Democrat Socialism, under both Republican and Democratic administrations. The evidence is in the facts. Any income-leveling, the taking from the "haves" and giving to the "have-nots" excludes certain individuals and institutions, creating privileged classes. The Founders foresaw this and made the establishment of privileged or any other classes strictly forbidden by the Constitution. Unfortunately, privilege and usurpation of economic power have existed throughout U.S. history. However, Socialism has done nothing to change this situation.

Thomas Jefferson wrote, "The government that governs least is one that governs best." As a constitutionalist, a prime author of this greatest blueprint for just government, he was not advocating anarchy at a moment of weakness, as has been charged in some quarters. This shows how many people have been misdirected by Socialist brainwashing. Jefferson wrote of a *strong* government under the Constitution centering the day-to-day activities on the state and local level. His aim was to avoid government meddling into the affairs of people and commerce which actually weakens government as we have seen.

Strong and firm regulation, as it reflects the Will of the People, is required by local government to keep people from infringing upon the rights of others in day-to-day activities of life and business.

Such legitimate regulation, coupled with the enforcement of the law, is the day-to-day business of government on the state and local level. It is impossible to have the central or federal government do this for the whole nation on an equitable and efficient basis. The Founders understood this very well and that is why they took such care to set up the federal government's powers as few and specifically limited by the Constitution. All other powers were to remain with the state and the people, as so clearly stated in the 10th Amendment. This amendment was the condition upon which most stated agreed to ratification of the Constitution which formed this federal union in the first place.

Let me now begin to tie up some loose ends. I've been concentrating on fiscal matters because that seems to be the peoples' control on government. Otherwise, there is nothing sacred about money. It is a commodity, like everything else, and is worth only what you want to use it for. As public funds go, the important thing is to respect the people who paid into the fund and spend in the way they intended the money to be used.

At a Washington conference in February of 1981, Mr. Reagan told governors that a major restructuring of the federal system to return power to the states "is a long-term dream of mine."

States were promised a radical retreat from intrusive federal regulations and mandates. The new block grants, Office of Management and Budget Director David Stockman promised, were but a first step toward cutting the "umbilical cord" and recognizing that "governors are just as concerned and compassionate and competent as the federal government." To keep the federal agenda on track, *Mr. Reagan set up a high-level administration task force to monitor and propose changes*. This was the Reagan administration taking the important first step and the *governors should have immediately responded by also setting up a task force to go to work on the process*.

Instead, they started taking pot-shots at the program, while giving general endorsement to the President's economic recovery plans, including budget reductions.

One of the most immature reactions by a politician was by Governor Jerry Brown of California. He stated, "We will vigorously oppose any attempts to shift costs to state and local taxpayers." Now where did he think the federal tax money was coming from in the first place? Governor Babbitt of Arizona joined in, saying, "The Reagan approach of 'trimming across the board' does not come to grips with the status of the federal system in which federal, state and local governments are tangled up in a mass of mutually recriminating and difficult intergovernmental problems." Obviously he doesn't even understand that is exactly what President Reagan's proposal is designed to eliminate.

Babbitt suggested the time was ripe for some radical "uprooting" to eliminate the federal presence entirely in some areas such as transportation, education and law enforcement. "If the governors have the fortitude," Babbitt went on, "to assume *some* basic functions as their responsibility, the federal government should be asked to assume total responsibility for income maintenance and transfer programs in which Washington operates directly with individuals."

And this should include, Babbitt went on, not only the areas in which President Reagan said there should be a safety net to support people in need — *Social Security, veterans' benefits, Medicare* and *aid for the aged and disabled* — it should also include those controversial, less popular programs of *Medicaid* and *Aid to Families with Dependent Children.*

So far, *Babbitt said, the Reagan administration has not responded to these 'sorting out' proposals*, except to say it believes states can more easily fashion cost economics in Medicaid and welfare — a long-held belief of the President.

The conclusions of Babbitt and others coming out of the Governors' conference would indicate that *they misinterpreted the thrust of the Reagan program* just as far as they misperceived the basic structure set up by the Founders to keep us from being mired in our present bureaucratic swamp. They used high-sounding rhetoric about swapping programs with the federal government and completely missed the point that *all of these social programs are Constitutionally forbidden* to the federal government for good reason. They are on the federal level *because of nearly five decades of mismanagement!* They are there because *previous governors took the path of least resistance* and cooperated with the federal government to take charge of program after program that should never have left state control. Now that it has become *too expensive, too inefficient,* and *threatens to bankrupt our whole country* almost everyone can see these past mistakes. Now the *governors should be working to help Reagan correct the system* in an orderly manner, instead of playing the usual game of 'confuse the voter' politics. Their proposals do get wide press coverage, which may be the real purpose they have in mind anyway!

The governors will do great damage to their own states if they don't change their attitude and get busy preparing their states for the federal transfer back to the states of all welfare, aid for aged and disabled, medical assistance for the poor, all government aid to education, transportation, law enforcement, etc. It is the Constitutional law of the land that they be handled by the states and local governments. *Legally they should never have left that level.* In all likelihood we would not be in our present crisis if they had remained on the state and local level. It is too late to bemoan what has happened but it is *not too late to agree that we have been traveling the wrong road* and now is the time to get back on the right course. If the governors really believe (as Babbitt stated) that the federal government is the correct place for "income maintenance, transfer payments, Medicare, aid to aged and disabled, Medicaid and welfare for destitute families and children," then they should lead the move to make it legal by putting through a Constitutional amendment to transfer those responsibilities to the federal government.

I suspect that they would find out the same thing that caused FDR's "brain trust" to start the transfer of responsibility from state to federal by deceit and usurpation rather than risk the amendment process. If these subjects had been explained to the people to the degree necessary to get a Constitutional amendment approved by three-fourths of the state legislatures, I doubt they would ever have passed.

Some programs do legally belong with the federal government. *Veterans' benefits should remain there* because they arose out of service in the *federal armed forces* and are part of the cost of our national defense which the Constitution instructs the federal government to handle. *Social Security* was sold to the people as a national retirement program. It was misrepresented as an actuarially sound plan where all people covered by it would put in their money during working years. The funds were represented as being placed in trust so that in retirement they would be there to draw on according to a schedule of payments. It is probably the greatest fraud in the history of this country because the trust funds were never set aside as promised and the system is bankrupt. *If this happened in a regular business enterprise, the company would now be in the hands of the bankruptcy court* and *the ones responsible* for the staggering losses of peoples' trust funds *would be serving long prison sentences in federal penitentiaries.*

The original perpetrators of the Social Security fraud have passed from the scene and so many have had a hand in continuing the misrepresentation to the public that responsibility is hard to place. After all, how would you prosecute 90 percent of all the federal politicians for the last 50 years?

We cannot look to the states for a solution to Social Security problems. The system was and is a federal boondoggle all the way. It has been the federal political vote-getter for decades and in the federal arena it should stay.

The most sensible solution and the most humane seemed to be advanced by Dr. W. Cleon Skousen: 1. To continue the present level of benefits to the present beneficiaries. They planned their lives on the government promise to pay and have a just claim that should be honored. Future payments should not be indexed to continue to rise, however because most recipients will receive far more benefits than they put in and the rest is coming back to them as a direct tax on the backs of the present taxpayers.

2. Those who have a few years to go and back to those who are just starting should all be given the option of taking back all the money that has been put into the system by their contributions and the matching contributions of their employers to put into other retirement plans of their own choosing. This would probably have to be taken in government bonds to allow the government a spread out time to repay. **3.** *If there is to be a national retirement plan offered in the future, it should have to stand the same scrutiny and follow the same rules for guarding the integrity of the funds that are required for business institutions who handle other people's funds. It should be optional, rather than mandatory.*

If a future retirement program that can serve the high purposes that were stated for the Social Security system could be equitably worked out and the federal government was lacking the constitutional authority the procedure for instituting it is simple. Refer it to the states in the form of a Constitutional amendment for ratification. If they deem it wise they will give approval.

It has been said many times in many ways that government is everyone's business. Over the years fewer citizens believed that, staying away from the polls and leaving the operation of government in the hands of "experts" and the politicians behind the "experts" because everything seemed so complicated. Experts *are* needed for technical matters of carrying out decisions. The basic decisions themselves are up to the people.

The major issue facing all the people of the United States is the continuation of the American political and economic system. The key factors are financial.

We must keep reminding everyone that the continuation of our economic and political system is at stake. Either we reduced government spending or we didn't make it.

If you have ever been faced with probable death, you know that your priorities suddenly change. The things that seemed important fade into insignificance in comparison to the real needs of sustaining life. For a while, at least, getting your share (or more) of the bounties, takes a back seat to the sheer joy of just being here to share at all! We have to shed the mentality of the sailor on the crew of a ship that struck an iceberg. Mac rushed to the bunk of his sleeping buddy Olley and yelled to the top of his lungs, "Olley, Olley, you've got to get up and help man the pumps. The ship is sinking." To which Olley replied, "Let'er sink. She ain't ours." Most of us know the ship is sinking and if she goes, we all go with her.

I believe that enough people are ready for the tasks ahead if we can elect leaders with enough guts to make those hard decisions. We cannot suddenly cut spending from 45 percent to 25 percent of national income. It must be done in a careful, step-by-step manner. Mr. Reagan is trying to slow the growth and start the reduction in spending. It may take four years — and it may take eight, but it must be followed to completion.

First we must list every program being engaged in by the federal government that is not authorized by the Constitution and set up a timetable to phase it out. At the same time we must set up a parallel timetable on the local or state levels of government to pick up the *needed* services and programs that are being phased out federally. At the same time, areas of federal taxation must be relinquished so that, where necessary, state or local taxes can be raised to cover the shifted burden.

In many cases, *the increase in costs on the state and local level will be less than half of what the cost was on the federal level* and the service will be faster and better. *Many programs and services will not be* picked up at the state or local level because the federal activity was completely unnecessary. In many cases *the cost of performing the services on the state or local level will be no greater than it presently costs* to put up with the red tape caused at the lower levels with the Feds handling the program.

One great discipline will come into play that was missing before. Since the service delivered by government and the *cost of that service will both be handled and paid for on the same level* there will be less chance *of waste and inefficiency*. That isn't to say that there isn't waste and inefficiency on the state and local levels of government also, but they are much less than on the remote federal level where detection and correction are much more difficult.

For those who are fearful that local and state government will not be as generous with the taxpayers' funds *in support of the needy of society* as the federal government has been, I say the truly needy need *not fear*. Certainly not I, nor anyone I know who would be in a position to affect those decisions, would deny public assistance to those who cannot support themselves. For the able-bodied who can, but will not work to support themselves, it is a different story. Those who can but won't work, have no right to live off the substance of those who do.

With policies that accomplish these goals, the cost of the whole framework of *social programs* will ultimately be *much lower as a whole,* and the lower burden on taxable wealth of the economy will guarantee a much *healthier* economy to support the necessary responsibilities of society.

CHAPTER TEN

Sound Monetary Policy — The Key

The survival of the United States, and, therefore, the free world, is so dependent on the nation's financial condition. The most fundamental order of business for government is to straighten out the monetary situation. Under the Constitution this is not only the proper but the vital role of federal government. The monetary system of the U.S. has been taken over by a group of private bankers and operates for the benefit of the few, often to the detriment of the rest of us. Very few people realize this and a much broader educational effort is necessary before it will be corrected. The Federal Reserve System is not federal at all.

A sound monetary system is necessary to have a free and prosperous nation of people.

The Founders knew this because the colonists had a lot of experience with unstable money and they knew that to have a stable economy they had to have a stable monetary system. Historically, there are two ways to make money stable.

One way is to relate all currency to precious metals which maintain a degree of stability in their value of buying power. The other is to maintain the same relative amount of money and credit in operation and only add to the money supply as fast as the growth of the gross national product will justify.

Part of the trouble leading up to the Revolutionary War was the resentment in the Colonies over having their own currency suppressed by the British Parliament and having to pay all taxes and contracts in gold or silver. It was so scarce that there was not enough in circulation to do an adequate job as the means of exchange. This created depressions and hardship.

After declaring their independence from England, the Colonies operated under the Articles of Confederation. To finance the war their Continental Congress issued paper money with no backing and far in excess of the value of the goods being produced. This created inflation so bad that the Continental dollar gradually reduced to less than one cent in value.

With the adoption of the Constitution, Jefferson hoped that the nation would go back to the earlier precedent of government issuing money based on a precious metal standard. The treasury could then set up branches for loaning money. All payments of interest would go to the general fund of the nation, thereby greatly reducing taxes.

The first of Jefferson's hopes were realized when the gold and silver standard was explicitly written into the Constitution (Article I, Section 10). Instead of adopting Jefferson's second part of the system, Alexander Hamilton, who was appointed Secretary of the Treasury, was able to convince President Washington to accept a private central bank on the order of European countries. Washington was swayed by the prospect of immediate credit resources. He was more fearful of the continuing inflation and chaos resulting from unstable money than he was in avoiding the pitfall of a private central bank controlling national monetary policy and currency. He took refuge in the fact that the charter would only last 20 years, giving the young nation time to get on its economic feet and develop political maturity.

But Jefferson considered the bank charter unconstitutional and warned:

> *"If the American people allow the banks to control the issuance of their currency, first by inflation, and then by deflation, the banks and corporations that will grow up around them will deprive people of all property until their children will wake up homeless in the continent their fathers occupied. The issuing power of money should be taken from the banks and restored to Congress and the people to whom it belongs."*

Dissatisfaction with the First Bank of the United States resulted in its charter expiring in 1811. However, the financial pressures of the War of 1812 resulted in demands for another central bank. The second Bank of the United States went into operation in 1816 with the U.S. government owning only five percent of the stock. Andrew Jackson was President when that charter expired and vetoed the act which would have extended it. What he saw was a small body of powerful bankers gradually building a financial empire at the expense of the American people. It was probably the most stormy and courageous act of his administration and the bank stockholders never forgave him.

The results of Jackson's refusal to continue the central bank proved he was correct, however. He got the government completely out of debt, ended up with a surplus of $35,000,000, and made $28,000,000 available to various states as loans.

When Abraham Lincoln became President, faced with the herculean task of financing a civil war in a divided nation, he found the treasury empty, necessitating the suspension of payments in gold by the national government. In addition to the legal tender of gold and silver coins minted by the government, there were more than 7,000 different bank notes issued by the 1600 state-chartered banks that circulated as paper money. He was shocked when the banks demanded 28 percent yearly interest for loans to the federal government in that time of crisis.

Instead of submitting to this usury, Lincoln convinced Congress to authorize the issuance of Government notes (called greenbacks) promising to pay "on demand" the amount shown on the face of the note. These were not issued as dollars but as notes authorized under the borrowing power of the Constitution in Article I, Section 8. I have one of those original greenbacks issued August 10, 1861 which states "Upon demand the United States promises to pay to the bearer One Dollar. Payable by the Assistant Treasurer of the U.S. at New York. Receivable in payment of all public dues." It was signed by the Register of the Treasury for the Treasury of the United States. Over the picture of President Lincoln it states "Act of July 17, 1861."

Lincoln wrote "...we finally accomplished it and gave the people of this republic the greatest blessing they ever had — their own paper money to pay their own debts." Financing the war on money issued on the credit of the government without interest was pure genius. It put no more money in circulation than would be done with the government going to the banks and paying them high rates of interest to put the paper money they created into circulation. Both would be inflationary if the supply of money increased more than the supply of goods and wealth, but with the government circulating its own money it saved the people the big additional expense of interest the bankers wanted to charge. It was a new way to finance a war without the bankers making large profits and gaining control of the actions of the government.

The banks attacked Lincoln and the greenbacks with a fury that never subsided. More scurilous stories, terrible cartoons, rude and downright vulgar jokes, and total falsehoods were circulated about Lincoln than any President in history. Had the "man of sorrows" not been of the sterling character he was he would certainly have cracked. Like Washington, he openly sought the help of the Lord and relied on His inspiration to guide the affairs of the nation through what appeared to be its destruction. Only after his assassination did the people of the land finally realize that they had been led by one of the great men of all times.

Some have advanced the theory that banking interests were the instigators of Lincoln's assassination because they feared he would lead the nation to complete independence from their financial domination and control. If he succeeded in America there was danger that the practice would also spread to Europe where their control remained complete. That is a question, like many others in the political intrigue among the nation, that will never be answered but the historic evidence is the banks never let up on Lincoln, and they were quite successful in their counter-attack on his greenbacks.

By various devious techniques Congress was induced to pass several bills which seriously distorted everything the President was trying to do. Circumstances finally forced him to issue bonds which the banks could buy with depreciated greenbacks and then charge the Government substantial interest rates on the bonds. Even Chase, the Secretary of the Treasury, joined the bankers in their demand that the power to issue the nation's money be returned to them.

In 1863, the Congress capitulated under the pressure of Wall Street bankers and authorized a privately-owned system of National Banks. Each bank was given virtually tax-free status and was allowed to print money.

At the end of the Civil War and after Lincoln's death, the major banking interests manipulated the economy back and forth in a series of boom and bust disasters that finally set the stage for what they were really after all the time: a central banking system that would give them total control of the nation's money, credit and economy. They accomplished the first step with the Glass-Owens bill that set up the Federal Reserve System on December 23, 1913. All National Banks had to join and State Banks could if they wanted to meet the requirements. Member banks provided the capital for the twelve Federal Banks by buying stock equal to three percent of their capital and surplus. No ownership is in the hands of the Government; it is completely owned by the private banking interests.

The promises made by the promoters of the Federal Reserve System made it sound like the nation was getting a real bargain, even though the powers they wanted were not legal under the Constitution. In return for the privilege of printing the nation's currency and serving as the government's bank they promised:

1. To operate entirely under the direction and control of the President and his appointees to the Board of Governors.
2. To pay interest to the government for the privilege of printing Federal Reserve notes as the nation's currency.
3. To perform many banking services for the government free of charge.
4. To manage the nation's money supply so that the American dollar would be protected and remain stable so as to keep prices relatively stable.
5. To take the United States out from the control of Wall Street.
6. To prevent any further depressions.
7. To be friend and helper of the farmer and helper of small business.
8. To keep the new system decentralized so that all twelve districts would have an equal say in the operation of the system.
9. To protect American interests against foreign monetary assaults.
10. To supervise and inspect the local banks and provide funds in case they were pressed by unexpected demands for payment and many

other equally good-sounding promises.

It is easy to see why Congress succumbed, even though, collectively, it should have known better. Let's see how these promises were kept.

The banks almost immediately escaped from keeping the promise to operate under the direction and control of the President and his appointees. They have influenced Congress to pass over 200 amendments to the original act that has completely changed the statutory profile of the Act. Even the Secretary of the Treasury and the Comptroller of Currency were eliminated from the Board of Governors. As a result, the President and the Congress found themselves helpless and unable to intervene when the Fed had acted against the interests of the American people and made billion-dollar decisions favorable to its banker stockholders.

Instead of paying interest to the federal government for the privilege of printing Federal Reserve notes as the nation's currency, they elected to use a loophole in the Act that gave them the choice to pay nothing. No interest has been paid and there is no way to force the Fed to do so.

Instead of managing the nation's money to maintain a sound dollar and stabilize prices, they have manipulated the dollar until today its purchasing power is worth less than 10 cents of the amount it was when the Federal Reserve took over. The Fed was behind the legislation to take the nation off the gold standard and, later, what was left of the silver standard.

Instead of fulfilling the promise to take the United States from under the control of Wall Street it reinforced Wall Street control. That promise was the biggest deception of all. The most powerful money trusts on Wall Street were the ones behind the passage of the bill and it was their money-managers who took over the Federal Reserve System as soon as the Act went into operation. The words of Congressman Charles Lindbergh in opposition to its passage were prophetic:

"This Act establishes the most gigantic trust on earth. When the President signs this bill the invisible government by the Monetary Power will be legalized...The worst legislative crime of the age is perpetrated by this banking and currency bill. The caucuses of the party bosses have again operated and prevented the people from getting the benefits of their own government..."

The fallacy of accepting their promise to prevent any further depressions was akin to the fallacy of hiring the fox to guard the hen house. A study of the events since passage of this Act would bring almost everyone to the same conclusion as that stated by noted economist Dr. Milton Friedman in his *Capitalism and Freedom*:

"I am myself persuaded, on the basis of extensive study of the historical evidence, that...the severity of each of the contractions (depressions) - 1920-21, 1929-33, 1937-38, is directly attributable to acts of commission and omission by the Reserve authorities and would not have occurred under earlier monetary and banking arrangements."

As this is written in 1982 we are experiencing the most

severe depression since the 1929-33 period, spread world-wide, and brought on mostly by the failure of the Federal Reserve System to keep its promises given by it to obtain control of our money and credit.

It is true that excessive government spending is the other culprit but if we had never veered from the Constitutional pattern and kept the money and credit of the nation in the hands of the federal government under the control of Congress, the money supply could never have been inflated to underwrite the deficit spending that has financed the explosive increases without our elected representatives having to take responsibility for the disastrous results before it had gone so far. As it has happened the trillion dollar debt we now owe mortgages the future of generations. The interest on this debt is more today than total federal expenditures were 16 years ago. It is transferring the economic life blood of this nation from the people who produce the wealth to the bankers who engineered and promised themselves into this position to control our money and credit.

Today we are in the depths of a severe depression caused jointly by the mismanagement of government and by the Federal Reserve System.

The promise that the Federal System would forever remain decentralized was broken in its first year of operation. The centralized money market in the United States was in New York and still is. The Federal Reserve Bank of New York dominated the other eleven districts and the decisions of supply and rates on money are made by the Open Market Committee usually without even consulting the other eleven district banks of the Fed.

The promise to protect American interests against foreign monetary assaults was also made to be broken. The big money interests which control the Federal Reserve have many foreign entanglements and have drained off large quantities of American resources to underwrite their interests abroad. The statement of Congressman Louis T. McFadden of Pennsylvania is even more descriptive of the situation today than when he made it during the Depression:

> *"Mr. Chairman, we have in this country one of the most corrupt institutions the world has known. I refer to the Federal Reserve Board and the Federal Reserve Banks, hereinafter called the Fed. The Fed had cheated the Government of the United States and the people of the United States out of enough money to pay the Nation's debt...The wealth of these United States and the working capital has been taken away from them and has been locked in the vaults of certain foreign countries for the benefit of foreign customers of these banks and corporations. So far as the people of the United States are concerned, the cupboard is bare."*

The promise to supervise and inspect local banks and to provide funds in case they were pressed by unexpected demands for payment has been partly kept and partly not. Some local banks have been helped in times of stress but most have not. It seems that those decisions are made on the basis of what best serves the purpose of the ones who control the Fed.

It may be difficult for some readers to realize the blatancy and the magnitude of the deception that took place to bring the Federal Reserve System into being. It is hard for all honest people to easily accept the fact that people who hold the high trust of positions in Congress and even Presidents of the United States would be co-conspirators, or foolish dupes, whichever was their part in handing over the monetary birthright of the people of this nation, to a group of powerful men bent on profit and control. To assist you in accepting this as a reality here are some additional quotes from men in high places who were involved on both sides.

Senator Owen, one of the sponsors of the Federal Reserve Act, spoke of relating to the provision originally in the Act that required the Federal Reserve to maintain stable money which would produce a stable price level:

> *"This mandatory provision was stricken out in the House under the leadership of Carter Glass. I was unable to keep this mandatory provision in the Bill because of the secret hostilities developed against it, the origin of which at the time I did not fully understand."*

Later he found out where these hostilities were coming from and said: "Under the administrations of Wilson, Harding, Coolidge, and Hoover, this Act diverted from its proper purpose on the advice of some who controlled the policies of a number of the largest banks." Senator Owen spent the rest of his life trying to get the Federal Reserve System repealed.

Representative William Jennings Bryan who, as Majority Whip, was instrumental in pushing the Federal Reserve Act through the House of Representatives wrote: "In my long political career, the one thing I genuinely regret is my part in getting the banking and currency legislation enacted into law."

In 1916, just three years after using his leadership as President of the United States to bring the Federal Reserve System into being, Woodrow Wilson wrote:

> *"A great industrial nation is controlled by its system of credit. Our system of credit is concentrated (in the Federal Reserve System). The growth of the nation, therefore, and all our activities are in the hands of a few men. ...We have come to be one of the worst ruled, one of the most completely controlled and dominated governments in the civilized world — no longer a government by free opinion, no longer a government by conviction and the vote of the majority, but a government by the opinion and duress of small groups of dominant men."*

Some historians have suggested that Wilson's early death came about because it broke his health to discover how completely he had been used by the powerful men who were responsible for his election to the Governorship of New Jersey and then President.

The warnings of a far more wise President, Abraham Lincoln, when he was thwarted in his attempt to initiate monetary reform and was forced to accept the National Bank Act in 1863 are fitting here:

> *"I see in the near future a crisis approach which*

> *unnerves me and causes me to tremble for the*
> *safety of my country. Corporations (of bank-*
> *ing) have been enthroned, an era of corruption*
> *in high places will follow, and the money power*
> *of the country will endeavor to prolong its reign*
> *by working upon the prejudices of the people*
> *until the wealth is aggregated in a few hands*
> *and the Republic is destroyed."*

Today it is easy to add "Amen" to his prophetic statement.

Another statement of President Lincoln is the best guide
for what we should do to correct the monetary end of our
problems. He said:

> *"Government possessing the power to create*
> *and issue currency and credit as money and en-*
> *joying the right to withdraw both currency and*
> *credit from circulation by taxation or other-*
> *wise, need not and should not borrow capital at*
> *interest as the means of financing governmental*
> *work and public enterprise. The government*
> *should create, issue, and circulate all the cur-*
> *rency and credit needed to satisfy the spending*
> *power of the government and the buying power*
> *of consumers. The privilege of creating and is-*
> *suing money is not only the supreme*
> *prerogative of Government, but it is the*
> *Government's greatest creative opportunity."*

It will take the joint effort of the states and the federal
government to solve the monetary problem. The Founders
had the right idea and put the correct powers in the Constitution but they did not implement it, as previously
stated. Hamilton, who engineered the first central bank

and convinced Washington to temporarily (20 years) take the course later admitted in a letter to a latter Secretary of the Treasury that the Government should "raise up a (money) circulation of its own" which would require that the Government no longer allow this important task of issuing money to be assigned to a private banking system.

The best plan I have seen to replace the Federal Reserve System with a sound monetary system has been suggested by Dr. W. Cleon Skousen, the respected scholar, lecturer, author and founder of The Freemen Institute.

Rather than try to summarize his plan and risk losing some of its meaning, I have secured his permission to quote from it.

> Here are some of the most important characteristics of a sound and honest money system which the Founders had in mind when they wrote the Constitution.
>
> 1 . Money should be recognized as nothing more than a unit of value designed to facilitate the exchange of goods and services. The right to *create* such a symbol therefore belongs to those who create the goods and services, meaning the people themselves. It is an inherent and inalienable right which they alone can delegate. In the Constitution the right to create the people's money was delegated to Congress.
>
> 2 . Once the right to create money is delegated to the people's representatives — the Congress — it is completely

unlawful for the Congress to give that right to a group of private bankers or "money-managers."

3 . It is the responsibility of the Congress to create a healthy dollar or unit of value which will maintain the same relative value from generation to generation.

4 . It is also the responsibility of the Congress to set up appropriate machinery to monitor the money supply so that it will remain in balance with the amount of goods and services being produced by the people. As productivity increases, the money supply should be increased, but only to the same extent. Congress has never provided the machinery needed to fix and maintain the value of money by regulating the supply in relation to goods and services.

5 . Machinery should also have been provided so that no powerful group of private money manipulators could suddenly drain off large portions of the money supply so as to cause a depression; or suddenly add to the money supply and thereby create sky-rocketing inflation. Either of these developments violates the responsibility of Congress to "fix" and maintain the "value" of the dollar as provided in the Constitution.

6 . It was also the intention of the founders that the issue of the dollar be locked into a designated amount of gold or silver. Throughout the history of modern man, precious metal has always been the

"money of last resort." Of course, people will ordinarily prefer to use paper money because it is so much more convenient to handle, but as Jefferson and others pointed out, it should be redeemable in gold or silver. And experience has taught us that U.S. notes should be redeemable in gold and silver at the prevailing market price rather than some arbitrary price fixed by statute. A statutory price allowed speculators to play havoc with our currency.

7. To safeguard the value of money against the manipulation of speculators, it is essential that the nation have such a large supply of precious metal in storage that no group of private speculators, either at home or abroad, can get a corner on the market and seriously alter the stability of the paper money which has been issued.

8. When a certain unit of value (the dollar) has been declared the official legal tender, no bank or individual should be allowed to make loans except in terms of monetary assets which are in actual possession or readily available. Fractional banking or loaning or "credit" backed by merely a fraction of the loan is inherently fraudulent and should be outlawed.

It has been known for many years that there is an escape from the present dilemma if a sufficient number of Congressmen can be induced to consider the source of the problem and the requirements for a solution.

The key to solving the problem is Section 31

of the Federal Reserve Act which provides that the government can buy back the stock from the Federal Reserve banks at any time, thereby acquiring all of the assets which have been accumulating in the Federal Reserve System during close to three-quarters of a century. At least two advantages would immediately result from this action.

First of all, the stock of the Federal Reserve banks would cost the Government less than a billion dollars whereas the assets of the Federal Reserve System are now nearly 200 billion. Most of these assets are in U.S. government bonds.

There is also another $100 billion being held in "reserve" for the member banks and practically all of these assets are in U.S. government bonds.

Secondly, the Federal Reserve system has obtained these billions in bonds without paying anything for them and therefore they can be taken back as part of the assets of the System without any obligation to compensate the stockholders for them. In order to understand how the Federal Reserve has been "buying" U.S. bonds without paying anything for them it is only necessary to follow the procedure in one of its purchases as an example:

Let us say the Federal Reserve applies to the U.S. Treasury for $500 million worth of bonds. The Treasury promptly prints up the bonds (Government IOU's) which require the American taxpayers to eventually redeem them at their face value plus a regular payment in interest. Now comes the surprise. The Federal

Reserve puts the bonds in its "reserve" fund and immediately treats these bonds as an asset. It then writes out a check to the Government based on the credit created by these bonds! In other words, nothing of value is surrendered to the Treasury for these bonds. It is simply a question of writing a check on the "credit" which the bonds themselves created.

When the member banks buy U.S. bonds, they follow the same procedure.

The important point to recognize here is that if the United States bought back the stock of the Federal Reserve System, the Government would also be entitled to all of the assets and "reserves" of the System including these bonds for which the Federal Reserve and its member banks paid nothing. These bonds could then be immediately cancelled since the Government would own them. They would not have to be redeemed nor would any further interest be due on them. It would be similar to a man who buys a company and finds that the assets include his own notes or IOU's. Through his purchase of the company he gets back these IOU's and can tear them up because he owes them to himself.

This procedure would wipe out approximately $200 billion worth of bonds belonging to the Federal Reserve System and another $100 billion worth of bonds in the "reserves" of the member banks.

There is another huge supply of U.S. bonds in the trust funds of various Federal agencies. These trust funds were originally set up to maintain a ready supply of emergency cash, but over the years these trust funds have been spent and replaced with U.S. bonds or IOU's. All of these bonds belong to the United States and should therefore be cancelled since they belong to the Government and should be considered redeemed, with no further interest due. This would account for another $100 billion or more which could be wiped off of the Federal debt, thereby bringing the total to approximately $400 billion in cancelled U.S. bonds which would practically cut the Federal debt in half. It would also cut the Government's annual interest payments in half.

All other outstanding U.S. bonds should also be redeemed and cancelled out as rapidly as the economy would permit. The United States would then be completely out of debt and by adopting the Founding Fathers' monetary formula the nation could stay out of debt forever.

Just as soon as the Government has acquired the stock in the Federal Reserve System, the Congress could proceed to take the steps which economists have been working out in progressive detail ever since the days of Jefferson, Jackson, and Lincoln. The basic requirements for the new monetary system should be carefully codified in an amendment to the Constitution. This amendment plus statutory implementation by Congress would need to provide for the following:

1 . Freezing the money supply at its present level to prevent any further deterioration by inflation.

2 . Setting up the necessary monitoring machinery to keep the supply of money within 3% of the Gross National Product

(goods and services) and use the price-index to provide a month-by-month correction so as to keep the ratio between the money supply and the GNP as exact as possible.

The only exception to the 3% restriction would be in time of war or an extreme emergency declared by Congress. The law should require that the excess money supply which had been pumped into the monetary system to meet the needs of the emergency, must be drained off through taxes of other means within five years so as to bring prices and the supply of money back into their original ratio. Only by this means will the savings of the people retain their buying power or "value" from generation to generation.

3 . Appointing the trustees in charge of the Federal Monetary System to permanent positions until they reach the age of 70. Their compensation should be substantial and not subject to being diminished during their term of service. The law should also provide for severe punitive action in addition to impeachment for any dereliction of duty on the part of these trustees or their supervisory officers.

There would also be a provision that no person could qualify as a trustee if the candidate or any members of his immediate family held stock or worked for any bank, loan association, or company which would benefit from the trustees' decisions and thereby represent a conflict of interest.

4 . New United States notes would be issued to replace the Federal Reserve notes and would be redeemable at the option of the government in either gold or silver. Congress would designate the gold and silver reserves required for domestic currency as well as for transactions in foreign exchange.

5 . The Open Market Committee of the Federal Reserve System would be abolished.

6 . No quantities of capital in excess of $5,000 could be taken from the country without the consent of the Trustees of the Federal Monetary System.

7 . All fractional banking by banks, loan associations and individuals would be strictly forbidden.

8 . Commercial banks and the public bodies of the individual States would be allowed to borrow funds from the United States Monetary System at 3% interest, these funds being allocated to each State according to its population unless Congress should deem otherwise. In the absence of a war or emergency, no such loans would be available unless they could be made within the ratio of balance required between the money supply and the GNP.

9 . Commercial banks and loan associations would not be allowed to loan any funds at interest in excess of 10%. Loans only could be made to the extent of funds borrowed from the Monetary System or its

tangible assets or the savings of its customers. Each bank would be required to maintain a dollar for dollar balance on all demand deposits (check book accounts) and would charge for services rendered in handling checks, notes or trusts for its customers. The present Federal Reserve branches would be taken over by the Federal Monetary System and would provide clearing house services as at present.

10. Borrowing by the Government would be forbidden. The right to create additional money for the people would be achieved by printing United States notes without interest and subject only to the limits of keeping the money supply in balance with the GNP. Issuing the people's money without paying interest and without borrowing would finally fulfill the formula of the Founders.

11. All commercial banks would be incorporated as entities of the individual States or territorial possessions. There would be no Federal banks or national banks. Nevertheless, the Federal Monetary System would have supervisory responsibilities over all banks and loan associations to verify their liquidity and promptly detect any fractional banking practices or other violations.

Here is what it could accomplish within a short time:

1 . Put the authority to issue the people's money back in the hands of Congress as

required by the Constitution.

2 . Allow money to be created as needed without borrowing or paying interest for it.

3 . Get the United States completely out of debt.

4 . Keep the money supply in balance with the productive quantity of goods and services so that the buying power or "value" of the U.S. dollar would remain approximately the same from generation to generation.

5 . Stabilizing the dollar would take the major risk out of putting savings in the bank, making industrial investments, buying a home, modernizing America's industry, investing in research and technology, stabilizing the stock market, and providing a realistic security for those retiring on a fixed income.

6 . It would prevent inflation. The money supply could not increase above 3% and the monitors would have the power to pull it back even from this minor amount of dislocation.

7 . It would also prevent depressions. Since the money supply would not be allowed to drop below 3% of the GNP at any time the trustees would closely monitor the price-index and if it revealed any tendency toward a slump, a new supply of money and credit could be immediately released to make up the difference.

8 . There also would be a tremendous reduction in Federal taxes. The 3% interest paid by commercial banks, public institutions, and loan associations would go directly into the United States Treasury. The States could then retain the needed tax resources to properly fulfill their Constitutional responsibilities.

9 . There would be practically no bankruptcy or collapse of banking institutions. State-incorporated commercial banks and loan agencies would no longer be subject to the boom-and-bust cycle. Nor would they be subject to the whims of the New York and European money trusts which have forced tens of thousands of American banks and loan associations out of existence during the past 200 years.

10. Commercial banks and loan associations could borrow money from the Federal Monetary System at 3% and loan it out competitively to the public at a higher interest rate providing it did not exceed 10%. They would charge a reasonable fee for servicing check accounts and maintain a dollar-for-dollar balance for all demand (check book) deposits so there would never need to be a "run on the bank" to recover these deposits. Savings, or time deposits, would also be the basis for loans at interest rates not exceeding 10% and the Federal Monetary System would monitor the accounts to make certain that every loan had been realistically underwritten by substantial collateral. The banks and loan associations would therefore operate like any other business

and make their profits from services rendered rather than gambling on fractional reserves and being required to participate in boom-and-bust economics which in thousands of cases have destroyed the reputation of banks and forced them out of existence.

11. The stabilizing of the money supply would go a long way toward stabilizing over-all prices. No longer would the farmer find himself paying rapidly inflated prices for equipment, fertilizer and fuel while his crop prices remained stagnant. No longer would manufacturers find themselves being forced to pay highly inflated prices for raw materials and labor thereby pricing themselves out of the world market.

12. For similar reasons the new monetary system would also greatly reduce the likelihood of strikes and tempestuous labor disputes.

13. A stable economy would greatly accelerate the velocity of business. However, studies show that the rapid turnover of money does not need to result in an inflationary cycle as many had supposed. It does produce a remarkable increase in goods and services but as this occurred the monitors of the Federal Monetary System would simply create additional money to keep the monetary supply in balance with the rising GNP.

CHAPTER ELEVEN

Bridging the Mainstream

I was in the hilltop home of Dr. and Mrs. Ted Winn in Prescott, Arizona, the night President Reagan gave his masterful State of the Union Address in January, 1982. I was ready to conduct a Constitutional seminar for a number of concerned citizens, and we watched the President on TV before beginning our discussion.

At the time I wondered whether or not the President would start to weaken on his programs to transfer power back to the states, reduce spending, reduce taxes, and rebuild our military strength, in the face of the deepest economic recession since the early 1930's. Within my lifetime all the Presidents have made bold pronouncements of noble intentions in the campaign to get elected. Later, when it came to carrying out the promises, the resolve seemed to disappear before the onslaught of entrenched Washington pressure groups that are determined to maintain the *status quo* as long as it benefits them and theirs.

To my great satisfaction, President Reagan showed no sign of buckling under the pressure. Instead he moved boldly ahead with details of 43 programs to be transferred back to the states and to provide the interim money for the states while they see which programs they really want to keep when the burden to pay for them would be directly on their shoulders. He spelled out details of the general outline he had given the Governors in February, 1981 in

Washington, and set up a 10-year guiding period for its accomplishment. I began to see real hope for the future when the President said he wasn't going to balance the budget on the backs of American taxpayers. He served notice that spending cuts, not continued tax increases, was the way to a balanced budget. This also was a direct response to those who accused him of wanting to balance the budget on the backs of the nation's poor when all he was trying to do was to "cut out the greedy so there will be enough for the needy."

To the great discomfort of Democratic Majority Leader "Tip" O'Neill, seated behind him, President Reagan laid out the course necessary to turn the direction of the nation away from further Socialism and back to the Balanced Center of the Constitutional system of government.

Everyone in our group was as elated as I was. Reagan was actually for real, not just another politician spouting rhetoric.

President Reagan understands what got us into the present crisis. He will stick to his principles as the only way to get us out. Now there is real hope for the future. If we can get him some help in the state capitols and more help in Congress there is really a chance to get this nation back on the Constitutional Balanced Center of freedom and prosperity. As came out in our discussion, we knew it wouldn't be easy. Some who inadvertently led us to the socialistic extreme still did not realize their errors. Others were still intent on central control so they could use the force of government to serve their selfish interests. But the revolution of the 80's was on and it was waiting for the people throughout the states to join battle.

For the past three years I had been spending a lot of volunteer time in assisting The Freemen Institute educate people on the basic principles on which the Founders set up this Constitutional Republic. I join those who feel that the majority of Americans are honest, decent, upright citizens who want to see the right things done but lack the knowledge to determine the correct course. I have seen thousands respond to the seminars and can see firsthand how completely the schools have neglected their duty to teach the Constitutional system of government. Had they done so the people would not have fallen for the false doctrine of Socialism and we would not be in the trouble we were in. It stands to reason then, that the way to awaken enough people to correct the problems is to educate them in correct principles...

Coming back from Prescott that night, my mind whirled with sequences of unfinished plans. For the past three months I had been getting my personal and business affairs in order so I could have the option of deciding what to do in 1982. I was so encouraged with Mr. Reagan's speech that it now looked like another race for the governorship might very well be worth the expense and effort. Now there was a real partner in the White House who saw the same things as I did — and had plans to get the nation back on the positive Constitutional track.

After the 1978 election I had made no effort to be involved politically. Although I was the titular head of the party, Republican Tom Pappas, the chairman of the state central committee, would have been much more comfortable if I wasn't around. I had opposed his election to the post and politics has its own scores to settle. Right after the election I had lunch with Pappas and suggested that inasmuch as the party had paid off the $150,000 in debts in Russ Williams' losing battle for Governor in 1974 that perhaps they would like to at least split the $135,000 debt I had in 1978. A lot of people, including me, felt that my campaign had furnished the momentum to keep the Democrats from sweeping the election and gave us some key state offices and control of the senate and added to the GOP majority in the house. Nothing was done at all by the party but a number of great supporters came through with almost $20,000 to help and I took care of the rest myself. One thing I agreed with Harry Truman on was when he said, "If you can't stand the heat, stay out of the kitchen." I didn't complain. That's politics!

Early in 1981 Pappas had announced with great public fanfare that he was appointing a committee to select a candidate for governor which could unite the party around one man to beat incumbent Bruce Babbitt. I watched this with great interest because this was my objective. Babbitt had proven himself a clever politician and certainly was more than a match for the Republican legislature. With the senate made up of 14 Democrats and 16 Republicans he had a veto-override-proof senate and he used the veto power to really whip the legislature, often to the detriment of the people and the state. He proved that he was really anti-business and strongly union, although he talked differently. He was a loyal and close supporter of President Carter and when he joined Rockefeller's Trilateral Commission it was visible proof that Babbitt had joined the "insiders' fraternity" so that he could be a cabinet member in the event of a second Carter term. It was no secret that Babbitt had high Washington aspirations. With the defeat of Carter, it appeared that the planned route would be a little different but Babbitt was working hard to be one of the national leaders in Democrat thought and action...

As my Pontiac rolled smoothly down out of the mountains, my mind raced back over the rest of the events of 1981. The Pappas selection committee finally narrowed the field down to Jack Londen, the GOP National Committeeman from Arizona, and Leo Corbet, the President of the State Senate. Londen had come to see me in late summer, just before the selection committee had its final meeting. He wanted my support and wondered what I wanted, to which I replied that I wanted nothing personally except good government. Jack was sure he had the committee votes to be chosen alone or at least jointly with Corbet. Both of them were reported to have made a pact to abide by the committee selection but when the majority voted for Corbet, Londen raised questions about the propriety of the committee procedures.

Aside from writing a letter to the committee members advising them to not do anything that could be construed as shutting out anyone else from running so their candidate wouldn't suffer from the effects of a perceived "backroom deal," I stayed away from any contact with the committee. I didn't agree with that way of choosing a candidate but I was hopeful they would get a good person we could all support, and one who could beat Babbitt and be a good governor. Both qualifications were necessary.

In September Leo Corbet came to see me and asked for my support. I asked him how he was going to beat Babbitt. He replied that he had been "down there" battling him in the senate for the last four years. I told him that it was the perception of a lot of people that he had done more to help put Babbitt's program through than battle him — and that he would find it hard to attack Babbitt's record overall when he had helped much of it become law! I then asked him to tell me what his program was and what he would do if he became governor. That would have a big influence on whether or not I could support him. He replied that he planned to put position papers together in October and see me then.

It was December when Leo came back, but again with no papers or plan. We had a friendly meeting; primarily, he wanted to inform me that crime was to be the big issue in the next legislative session and he had little to say about a program as governor.

By this January night, Leo had been alone in the field for five months as the committee choice for governor but had no program, and as far as I could see, he was making very little progress. I had been concluding my business affairs to give me the option to enter the race if it was deemed necessary, yet I was putting this off and found myself not really wanting to get to the point of deciding "yes" or "no." I hesitated to conclude that if Mr. Reagan was to get help from the Governor of Arizona, it would have to be me to do it, but it looked like that was the case. I was going to have to fish or cut bait.

As could be expected, the Democrats attacked Mr.

Reagan's speech and the network newsmen told their version of what he had said and what it meant. In spite of the detractors, it appeared to me that mainstream America was with the President. Most people know that we didn't get into the mess we were in all at once and that we wouldn't get out overnight and without some pain. The important thing was that Mr. Reagan wasn't stampeded by immediate economic problems into changing his long-term plans.

Finally we appeared to have a man in the White House who was leading the way in Washington to return the power to govern back to the states. It was now up to the states to get organized and assist the transition from the state and local levels. Unfortunately, there were no governors stepping forward to lead in this effort. Most cautiously raising questions. No one, according to the Associated Press, was ready to be unqualified in support of the plan. Some feared it would cause them to have to raise state taxes and others thought the governors might come up with some alternative state-federal swap plans. It was a scene we have witnessed so often in recent decades. We had few leaders because they had not done their homework, and did not really understand the Constitutional system they took an oath to uphold. They were accustomed to playing cautious politics in which you watch what others are doing before making your move. After all, it's good politics to wait and make sure you aren't out there by yourself. It may be good politics but it sure isn't going to correct past mistakes!

The reaction of Arizona Governor Bruce Babbitt was pragmatic politics at its best. Using generous words of praise he led the casual reader in Arizona, where Mr. Reagan was very popular, to believe that he was in full accord with the President's plan. He "thinks it deserves a chance." Then he cautiously suggested that there were some decisions yet to be made about which programs should be handled on state level and which on federal level. Actually he was attempting to put himself in the lead of the federal welfare staters who were determined to put all welfare on a federal level and keep the less expensive education, law enforcement, and roads on the state and local levels. This was the usual liberal trick that worked so often over the previous 30 years. When you are in trouble, don't go back and correct the trouble at its roots. Just change it in some way that you can point to as a solution and the people won't catch up to the fact that you haven't solved anything until after the next election!

In a January 28th article appearing in the *Washington Post,* Babbitt was far more candid. Being among his liberal peers on the Washington scene he again praised the President for his effort but took him to task on the substance.

Babbitt said, "We must develop a national agreement on which programs should be run in Washington and which should be left to state and local government." (The Constitution specifies what should be federal and all others should be state or with the people. All of these being discussed are state and local.) Babbitt continued: "The major issue will be entitlement programs, such as Medicaid, AFDC and food stamps. The nation's governors have long argued that these programs are properly a national responsibility. When the unemployment rate is 16 percent in Michigan but only 5.5 percent in Texas, it is manifestly unfair to ask Michigan residents to shoulder welfare created by national economic policies. The President has forseen this issue and proposed a disingenuous swap: federalize Medicaid to induce state acceptance of welfare and food stamp responsibilities. *That proposal should be rejected.*" From this is was very clear that he and any other governors he was attempting to be spokesman for did not realize why we were in the mess that engulfed us. The federal "entitlement programs," as Babbitt called the welfare handouts, had almost bankrupted the nation. With the federal government making the rules and not allowing the states much authority except to be the dispensing agents, inefficiency and graft had become so rampant that the spending was out of control; when the source of funds was far removed from the responsible parties who dispensed the largess there was little restraint on their use.

The very word "entitlements" as used by Babbitt has the connotation that "free" federal funds is money that the recipients are entitled to without any concern for who the money was taken from and why anyone is "entitled" to the substance that someone else had to labor to earn. It is a complete repudiation of the Founders' success formula wherein they so carefully guarded against the federal government getting into any of these state and local responsibilities. They had seen the same abuses as we see today, ripen into welfare statism in previous civilizations and finally destroy the vitality and strength of everyone who took that course. When you get more people on the "entitlement rolls" than you have on the producers' rolls, the incentive to produce gradually disappears. When there are not enough producers to feed the rest, the system collapses into a chaotic upheaval with tragic results for all.

Rather than enter into a prolonged debate of which programs should go where, we should go to our proven success formula and put all welfare, food stamps, AFDC, Medicaid, Medicare and personal subsidies of every kind on the state and local level. Pensions or disabilities emanating from federal government service should be the only exceptions. Even if economic conditions are good in Texas and bad in Michigan, there is no justice in taxing Texans to pay Michigan's bills. If conditions are so much better in Texas than in Michigan, there is nothing to stop people in Michigan from going to participate in those better conditions in Texas. Furthermore, the burdens created by national economic policies that Babbitt referred to would also be erased when we straightened out the system because the federal government will no longer control the marketplace. In its place will be a free market that will create a prosperous climate to provide an abundance for all able-bodied who will work. There will also be ample funds on the state and local levels to give proper care to all the truly needy who cannot take care of themselves.

The next point of the Babbitt *Washington Post* article was the same political doubletalk we have heard so often, designed to build minority voting constituencies. He wrote: "The President must convince us that his program is not simply a front for neglecting civil rights and abandoning the hard-won gains of blacks and other minority groups. Many federal assistance programs, notably education, were created to provide equal opportunity for minority groups victimized by racial discrimination....Nevertheless, there may be better ways than scatter-gun grant programs to ensure continued progress in civil rights." There was nothing in President Reagan's actions that warranted this accusation. It appeared to be the usual liberal finger-pointing tirade based on the premise that an accusation repeated often enough will finally be accepted as a fact. The Babbitt-type liberals would continue to try to use minorities and civil rights as the ploy to concentrate more federal control over most activities in our lives.

Babbitt's third point..."The president must forthrightly address the issue of inequities among states in per capita taxing power and program need....Alaskans, who pay virtually no taxes and receive dividend checks each year, may be already getting too much federal aid; in Mississippi, with the lowest per capita income in the country may well be a case for supplemental federal aid." Again the bleeding heart theory of using the federal government to take from the haves and give to the have-nots. That is not the federal government's legal and rightful role. Indeed no government has that legal right and it will do nothing but confuse the issues at hand to get a new national debate going in this field.

Babbitt's questions and statements were but a restatement of the New Deal, Fair Deal, New Frontier, and Great Society of Roosevelt, Truman, Kennedy and Johnson with a little of Eisenhower and Nixon thrown in for good measure. We were trying to extricate ourselves. The rule of men has led us astray. It was time to follow Mr. Reagan's lead and get back to the rule of law as clearly defined in the Constitution.

Let those who want further experimentation with the social programs on a federal level make their proposals to the nation in the form of amendments to the Constitution.

If they can prevail, it will become the law of the land and we will all agree. Meanwhile, they should have the good grace to uphold the Constitutional law of the land and follow the President in his moves to restore the government to its rightful and legal activities.

For many years I have been trying to refine a plan down to one instrument that would solve all the problems in one fell swoop. I believe we now have it and that now the climate is ripe to try it out. I do not claim to be the author, merely the compiler. It is the result of the work of many, and is simple as are all truths, leaving ample room for debate and change.

STATES' BILL OF RIGHTS

The most rapid and simple way to put the plan into effect is for Congress to pass and refer it to the states for ratification as the 26th Amendment to the Constitution known as the States' Bill of Rights. If Congress fails to act quickly, Article V of the Constitution states…"on application of the Legislatures of two-thirds of the several states, shall call a Convention for proposing amendments, which, in either case shall be valid in all intents and purposes, as a part of this Constitution, when ratified by the Legislatures of three-fourths of the several states."

Preamble: Inasmuch as there have been many laws passed by Congress, legal decisions given by the Supreme Court having the effect of making laws, the executive orders given since the ratification of the Constitution that seem to have no foundation of authority in the Constitution, it is necessary to end the confusion of interpretation by the passage of the following amendment to the Constitution which shall be known as the States' Bill of Rights:

1. The President of the United States shall appoint, with the advice and consent of the Senate, a five member commission named the CONSTITUTIONAL COMPLIANCE COMMITTEE. Terms of office shall be for five years except the terms of the first committee shall be staggered from 1 to 5 years so that one member position shall expire each year. The sole duty of this committee shall be to review all activities of the federal government and make an annual report to the President, Congress, the Governor of each state, and the Legislature of each state, of all activities of any kind being engaged in by the federal government that is not authorized by the Constitution of the United States as amended, and recommend the time that should be allowed to phase out and discontinue all unconstitutional activities.

2. Congress shall pass all legislation necessary to direct the executive department to bring the activities of the federal government into compliance with the Constitutional Compliance Committee Report within one year of each annual report. The failure of Congress to implement the Report within the prescribed time shall be sufficient proof that any member of Congress who has delayed or knowingly impeded the compliance in any way, has violated his or her oath of office and shall be removed from office within 30 days.

3. In the event Congress does not pass all the legislation

necessary to implement the Report within the prescribed time the states may do so with the passage of resolutions approved by a majority of the states.

4. Within one year from the effective date of this amendment, Congress shall repurchase all the stock of the Federal Reserve Banks as provided in Section 31 of the Federal Reserve Act.

   (1) Freeze money supply at present level.

   (2) Set up monitoring machinery to keep the money supply within three percent of the Gross National Product and appoint trustees to oversee the operation.

   (3) Issue United States notes to replace Federal Reserve Notes, redeemable in gold or silver at the market price at any time.

   (4) Government borrowing is forbidden.

   (5) All banks become state banks but the federal system still supervises currency clearance and such other housekeeping functions.

5. The 16th Amendment is hereby repealed.

6. All federal lands shall be deeded to the respective states except the National Parks and federal land and buildings necessary to carry out the constitutional activities of the federal government.

7. Participation in the Social Security System shall be voluntary hereafter.

8. The 'General Welfare' wording of the Preamble will not hereafter be interpreted as extending the power of the federal government into any area or power not specifically named in the body of the Constitution and its amendments.

Even before they see this proposal I can almost hear the screams of opposition from those who have had a hand in changing the American Republic into a socialistic superstate over recent decades. To answer their cries of derision and accusations that we want to take the country back to Neanderthal times, I merely say that the jury is finally in on both systems. We have ample historic records to chart the results of both Socialism and Free Enterprise economics. We have ample historic records to chart the progress of a nation ruled by the Rule of Law under a Balanced Center Constitution vs. those ruled by the "Rule of Man" through the ages and so much in evidence today.

To any detractors I merely say in advance, let us both take our proposals before the people of this great land and let them make the decision through their influence on elected representatives. Let us not stifle debate on this vital subject; let us take it into every corner of the land and have a total review of our foundation, our history, and our present circumstances. I have no fear of which course the people will choose if given the opportunity. The wise and prophetic words of President Thomas Jefferson should guide us: "I know of no safe depository of the ultimate powers of the society but the people themselves; and if we think them not enlightened enough to exercise their control with a wholesome discretion, the remedy is not to take it from them, but to inform their discretion by education."

Let us be men and women of good will and present our points of view to the people of the land with facts and records but not with name-calling and recrimination. Time is running out for America. We are a nation in deep trouble and because of our troubles the whole world is in trouble, such is our place in the affairs of the world. Indeed we owe it to all peoples in the world and to generations yet unborn to solve our present problems quickly and properly. Above all we owe it to ourselves and to our children to right the wrongs that the present generation has inflicted on our political, economic, and social institutions. Come Back, America!

CHAPTER TWELVE

The Agenda for
Come Back, America

*The powers delegated by the proposed Con-
stitution to the Federal government are few and
defined.. Those which are to remain in the State
governments are numerous and indefinite.. The
powers reserved to the several States will extend
to all the objects which, in the ordinary course
of affairs, concern the lives, liberties, and pro-
perties of the people, and the internal order,
improvement, and prosperity of the State.*

*Federalist Papers, No. 45
by James Madison, 1788*

With the powers, rights, and responsibilities flowing
back to the states in all the areas listed by Madison (above
quotation) the transition will be more revolutionary in the
states than in the federal government. In the federal
government's case, some programs will be transferred intact and others will just disappear. To make it a smooth
transition it is important to establish an agenda for all
parties (federal, state, counties and cities) to go by.

President Reagan committed his Administration to a
10-year transition period but I believe most necessary
changes can be made much quicker if all parties honestly
cooperate on carrying out a joint agenda for the transition.

The most important part of the transition agenda is that

it be put together by representatives of all levels of government affected and that a strict time limit like 90 days be imposed on the agenda's completion. Inasmuch as the federal government is divesting and the other governments are receiving, I suggest that the President extend an invitation to all states to send one transition agenda member to represent the state and one each from each state to represent the cities and counties. This would total 50 state representative members, 50 county representatives, and 50 city representatives. I suggest that the President then appoint 50 members from the federal government and designate one of them with cabinet level-rank to preside and organize the proceedings. The chairmanship should be rotated each week between the federal and state delegates.

Some will oppose the return of government to its lawful level on the grounds that some of the social advances of the recent decades will be lost in state administration. This fear is entirely unwarranted because the federal government will have lost none of its legally-constituted authority to see to the protection of Constitutional rights throughout the nation. The difference here is that the federal government cannot inject itself into issues of entirely local concern as it has illegally done in the past. The protection of rights is a two-edged sword and the federal government in the past has infringed on the rights of one under the guise of protecting others.

The lawful federal power to correct injustice is still intact and can be appealed to at any time. No legal power now held by the federal government will be rescinded in the area of civil rights, voting rights, minority rights, etc. In strengthening the right and just federal power, great savings would accrue because there are now vast federal bureaus and commissions of nebulous value and they can be phased out.

As a result, the states will have the freedom to be responsive to the people and deliver more and better service at lower cost. People who are concerned with peculiarities of their own locality can do a much better job of problem-solving for a state or district than they can under federal rules that must fit the entire land. In many cases, these improvements can be delivered by the same people who are now in place just to respond to the federal dictates.

Safety regulations can be handled better within the state. Arizona does not need the same regulations in its copper industry, for example, as does Michigan for its auto manufacturing plants. There is no greater wisdom on the federal than on the state level in these matters. All too often regulations from Washington have been imposed by a small minority which used the federal power to force its will on others with no real benefit and often with great damage. On the state level, a mistaken rule can be corrected easily; on the federal level change is often impossible or at the very least a cumbersome process. Here, again, there is little likelihood of increased costs for the state. The time and money spent within the states just to try to keep within federal requirements will usually be enough for the states to do the job themselves — and do the job better.

Environmental protection offers an excellent example of the advantages of state vs. federal control. The effect of making rules for the whole diverse nation on environment has been disastrous to the economy and has not provided any more protection to the environment than could state regulation. If the states were doing the job, why did the federal government step in? Because minority interest groups asked the government to do so. Only through the federal bureaucracy could the so-called "environmentalists" impose their will on the people.

Using Arizona's copper industry as an example, the federal regulations have made it difficult for Arizona copper to compete in the world market. I lived in the copper-producing town of Ajo for four years. I never heard of anyone getting sick or contracting any disease because of smelter smoke. Then the federal EPA officials decided that they must save the people of Ajo from the terrible effects that no one was complaining about. The result was an initial expenditure of $50 million on the smelter and a reduction of efficiency which I am told increased the cost of producing copper by approximately 15 cents per pound. With copper priced between 70 to 90 cents per pound, that is a severe penalty to pay. The added cost put Arizona copper at a great price disadvantage with foreign metals that pay no such penalties. This example can be applied to thousands of situations across the nation.

If the states can take control of environmental protection the rules can be laid down to fit each locality and industry in that locality. In the case of Arizona copper production, there was justification in insisting that the producers take some corrective action to clean up the air. As near as I can ascertain, this could have been done for three to four cents per pound cost in production on the average, if the state could have worked out the rules for each smelter. The saving in cost of approximately 10 cents per pound could have saved several thousand miners' jobs and grievous damage to the economy of Arizona.

EPA rules have slowed so much development and added so much to production costs that the entire economy has suffered more than can even be accurately calculated. It is true that there was needed action in this area. We all want to protect the air, water, and overall cleanliness of our environment but within realistic bounds and not at the cost of our livelihood. There can be a happy medium where we have reasonable protection of the quality of our surroundings and still keep the cost effective in relation to results. That can be done on the state and local level efficiently and quickly, again reducing the overall cost to the taxpayers. State and local costs will go up little, if any, and a huge federal bureaucracy will disappear from the federal budget.

Education is one of the most counter-productive areas of federal government intervention. Federal funds have never been as much as 10 percent of the amount spent by the states and local governments on the educational system but the bureaus have exercised vast controls that have actually increased educational costs in excess of the amount provided by the federal treasury. In the opinion of educators I know federal intrusion has been the principle cause of deterioration in the quality of education in America. To meet federal guidelines administrative staffs have had to be greatly expanded. Classroom teachers have had to spend too much of their own time complying with federal rules and this has reduced their effectiveness in their primary purpose of teaching. The federal dictates in curriculum had created much waste in the demands of things being taught that are not in the best interests of the students as judged at the local level.

With the federal government out of the local picture, a vast amount of federal money will be saved and state and local costs will reduce the taxpayers' burden by more than the amount no longer being received from federal sources. The quality of education can be expected to increase because more of the money can go to the classroom teachers and less to administrative overhead.

Federal operation of the welfare system is perhaps our largest disaster. The liberals will decry any proposal to reduce welfare rolls but necessity is forcing decisions to be made in this direction. The path created by federal intervention is strewn with the wreckages of program after program that was to solve the problem. The result has been to have two overheads to do one job. The federal bureaucrats are no wiser than state administrators. There is no money raised by the federal government that wasn't taken from the taxpayers of the states. Once again the intervention of the federal government into this state and local concern has illustrated the fallacy of trying to make national rules to apply to all localities. The actual delivery of welfare services has always been state and local. Why have federal rules?

We all agree that we should share the responsibility for helping members of society who cannot care for themselves and who do not have members of their own family who can and will accept the responsibility for their care. These can be cared for without federal dictates. Local people are probably more compassionate, and surely not less so, than federal administrators.

In addition to being the legally-correct level for all medical and welfare service deliveries, the state and local administrators can do a more efficient job without outside interference. Each state should be able to make its own rules and solve its welfare problems within the parameters of what is best for all members of society. We have tolerated the federal social planners' redistribution-of-the-wealth schemes all too long to the detriment of both the producers and the non-producers in our society. It is time we again listened to the wise counsel of our Founders who had studied the mistakes of the civilizations of all ages and took great care to guard us from repeating them.

Benjamin Franklin wrote:

> *To relieve the misfortunes of our fellow creatures is concurring with the Deity; it is godlike; but, if we provide encouragement for laziness, and supports for folly, may we not be found fighting against the order of God and Nature, which perhaps has appointed want and misery as the proper punishments for, and cautions against, as well as necessay consequences of, idleness and extravagance? Whenever we attempt to amend the scheme of Providence, and to interfere with the government of the world, we had need be very circumspect, lest we do more harm than good.*

Federal vs. state ownership of the land may sound like it is an issue in the Western states only — but the principle is of importance to all states.

In the original states, there was no issue raised over the land because it belonged to the states and the federal government only owned what was needed for its legally-constituted activities of government. When some of the states in the West were admitted to the Union, the federal government did not recognize the state sovereignty over the land within the borders of the new member states. This did not give the Western states entrance into the Union on an equal footing with all others and presented a legal question that has erupted in recent years. I will not solve it here but it is one of the important points that needs to be addressed as we get the federal government to confine its activities to those allowed by the Constitution.

Getting the federal government out of the land business is just as important as getting it out of all the other areas of state and local concern. Arguments that only federal bureaucrats are qualified to operate vast lands, within many states have no more validity than they have for welfare, education, environment, safety, law enforcement and a myriad of other areas. National parks and federal government installations are justified; I cannot see where any other federal land business is. The federal government should complete the unfinished business of granting statehood to all states in which it withheld land, and deed all other lands, except parks and needed installations, to the respective states within whose borders the land lies.

I know that there will be great cries of opposition from environmentalists and other self-appointed guardians of the public good. They will continue to advance the dogma that only the federal government can keep the greedy from raping the public domain. They will say state governments are corrupt and can be bought off by greedy speculators without acknowledging the fact that remote Washington and layers of bureaucracy are what invite abuse. The environmentalists fail to recognize that the people most interested in protecting the environment are those who live in it.

I quote Thomas Jefferson in this regard. In a letter to Gideon Granger on August 13, 1800 he wrote:

> *Our country is too large to have all its affairs directed by a single government. Public servants at such a distance, and from under the eye of their constituents must, from the circumstance of distance, be unable to administer and overlook all the details necessary for the good government of the citizens, and the same circumstances by rendering detection impossible to their constituents, will invite the public agents to corruption, plunder and waste. And I do verily believe, that if the principle were to prevail, of a common law being in force in the U.S. (which principle possesses the general government at once of all the powers of the State governments, and reduces us to a single consolidated government), it would become the most corrupt government on the earth.*

We have ignored that warning and allowed too much of what Jefferson cautioned against to happen. Certainly we have ample evidence now to prove to all people of good intention that governmental responsibility as described by Madison at the beginning of this chapter is the more efficient, least expensive, makes us the most prosperous, and gives us the greater freedom than the Socialistic system imposed on us in recent decades.

This chapter was not an attempt to set up a complete agenda for the states and local governments nor to discuss each area involved. Setting the true agendas will take careful deliberation by legislatures, state executives, county supervisors and administrators, city councils and administrators, with plenty of citizen participation. Here, I intended to bring up the basic principles and reasoning behind the needed actions.

President Reagan has made the first big move. If the revolution of the 1980's is to be successful in restoring our Constitutional system of government and bring back the prosperity and freedom we formerly had, we must move quickly ahead on the state and local levels to meet the Reagan administration in full partnership. It can only happen through cooperation among all parties. Time is of the essence.

Epilogue: The Fabulous Future

Getting back to my boyhood again, I remember my first proud achievement was being able to skip a flat stone across the pond. I could make it skip four or five times and more, sometimes bouncing the stone across the water all the way to the other side.

In a way, this is what I have done with this writing, skipping stones across a great sea, touching some points and missing others, in order to reach the opposite shore. The task has been a humbling one but necessary to express ideas and the processes and circumstances that were behind the development of those ideas.

Looking back, I have tended to sound negative and critical when, in reality, I am proud of America's achievements and hold high hopes for the nation and the world it will lead into the future. If I can reduce my criticism of the present order of government to one statement it would be that centralized power expresses a fear of the future as reflected in the lack of confidence in people to guide their own destinies. I hold no such fear and I don't think the majority of Americans do, either.

Doing what we must to remain a free people, putting aside false notions of government and rebuilding on the solid bedrock of the Constitution, we have a fabulous future ahead of us.

By reducing the cost of government from the present 45 percent of national income to 25 percent or less we can free up vast amounts of money now used to maintain the *status quo* to build new industry and culture.

Getting the monetary system out of the manipulative control of a few bankers and back into the hands of federal government where it belongs will eliminate inflation; wipe out half of the tremendous national debt; make money available at 5 percent interest or less. It would bring an end to the economic disasters brought on by artificial contraction and expansion of the money supply. This will achieve a new, high level of confidence in the economy and assure the stability of money from generation to generation, thus stimulating capital investment.

Reducing non-democratic, centralized control of our lives by bureaucracies will eliminate the power of selfish interests and godless social planners who "know what is best for us" and "protect us from ourselves." This would give us room to breathe, to expand, to explore, to pursue our dreams; to enjoy.

By getting the functions of government back to the level where they belong — the people level — we can reduce costs of government while increasing services and efficiency. Government would be responsive to the people, rather than making the people responsive to the will of those who rule governmental bureaucracies.

People who need help will be helped and at a higher level than they are at present while those who are capable of helping themselves will be given a place in an ever-expanding economy. Those who are helped will be helped and no strings will be attached to assistance.

The chain reaction to these positive actions will raise the United States and the people of the free world to new heights. With the alleviation of want and misery, world unrest would be reduced; with a strong America the chances of world conflict would be lessened.

I think it was Buckminster Fuller, the architect and technological visionary, who said that the frontiers of achievement for mankind are as limitless as the universe. I believe that. Yet there are those among us who would limit our vision to the narrow confines of their own limited thoughts and ideas as though there was nowhere else to go, nothing to do — that we are trapped to relive the present over and over again according to their dictates.

Scientists are now starting to learn what the Sacred Writings of all people through the ages had taught us: Life didn't evolve and stop to go on a downward spiral. The earth is young and fresh, constantly changing and renewing itself. If history was a day, the computer would have been fashioned a split second ago; atomic energy discovered a few seconds ago; the invention of power generation, reciprocal engine, flight, electronic communication, mere minutes ago.

What more can we do in the next few minutes of the next historical day?

List the great discoveries and inventions of the past century — medical developments, art, literature, economic and social science, biology and geology — and you will find the majority to be related to the names of Americans and adopted Americans. This was no mere coincidence, an accident of geography or the bounty of nature, as has been claimed. America was the creation of a free people who produced more to create more with a zest for life and without fear for the future.

Until the recent decline, Americans did all of this under the guidance of God and the Constitution as set down by the Founders.

Let's return to the Constitution and get back to work.